On the Road to Victory

On the Road to Victory

The Rise of Motor Transport with the
BEF on the Western Front

Michael Harrison

Pen & Sword

MILITARY

AN IMPRINT OF PEN & SWORD BOOKS LTD.
YORKSHIRE – PHILADELPHIA

First published in Great Britain in 2019 by
PEN AND SWORD MILITARY
An imprint of
Pen & Sword Books Ltd
Yorkshire – Philadelphia

ISBN 978 1 52675 043 3

Typeset in Times New Roman 11/13.5 by
Aura Technology and Software Services, India
Printed and bound in the UK by TJ International

Pen & Sword Books Limited incorporates the imprints of Atlas, Archaeology,
Aviation, Discovery, Family History, Fiction, History, Maritime, Military,
Military Classics, Politics, Select, Transport, True Crime, Air World,
Frontline Publishing, Leo Cooper, Remember When, Seaforth Publishing,
The Praetorian Press, Wharncliffe Local History, Wharncliffe Transport,
Wharncliffe True Crime and White Owl.

For a complete list of Pen & Sword titles please contact
PEN & SWORD BOOKS LIMITED
47 Church Street, Barnsley, South Yorkshire, S70 2AS, England
E-mail: enquiries@pen-and-sword.co.uk
Website: www.pen-and-sword.co.uk

Or
PEN AND SWORD BOOKS
1950 Lawrence Rd, Havertown, PA 19083, USA
E-mail: Uspen-and-sword@casematepublishers.com
Website: www.penandswordbooks.com

Contents

Acknowledgements

I would like to express my thanks to the following people who were of enormous assistance throughout the whole process of bringing this work from the kernel of an idea through to publication.

Lyn Gregson and the late Rex Gregson for yet again being kind enough to allow use of their extensive library. Tim Pierce and all the staff of the College Hall Library, RAF Cranwell for the kind invitation to use one of the world's great libraries. The director and staff of the Royal Logistics Corps Museum for the assistance and guidance given when this work was the subject of a dissertation. Professor Gary Sheffield and Doctor Spencer Jones for their encouragement in the study of motor transport with the British Army on the Western Front.

Richard Shaw of 'Culture Coventry', Elisabeth Chard-Cooper and Bob Holt of Coventry Transport Museum for allowing me to become acquainted with their very fine Maudslay lorry of First World War vintage and the considerable time they gave up from their working day to explain the workings of the Maudslay. The noted historian Richard Pullen who willingly shared his encyclopaedic knowledge and also provided images of First World War vehicles.

Matt Jones, Heather Williams and all the staff of Pen & Sword for their decision to go forward with the original idea for the work and their subsequent encouragement to see the project through to fruition. Irene Moore for her wealth of experience in editing and publishing and her infinite patience.

To my family who always and without fail encourage Dad in his schemes, however wayward they might seem. Finally, and most importantly, my dear wife Joyce, the multi-role administrator who in the blinking of an eye became the pilot who steered the ship when the storms of ideas-famine threatened to drive us on to a rockbound shore.

My sincere thanks to all of you.

Michael Harrison MA

Tho' ours is not the kind of job,
    That leads to much promotion,
We try to do our little bit,
    And Tommy, I've a notion,
Wont want for much, if we can help,
    To give him good supply,
And if we don't always succeed,
    You bet, at least, we try.

From one of the

A.S.C.

A.S.C. Army Service Corps.

Introduction

Transport and Supply
(logistics in modern terms)

Wars are won and lost on the logistical capacity of the belligerents to supply the needs of their forces as and when required with the means to prosecute the war. The great Chinese military thinker, Sun Tzu writing circa 500BC declared: *'When a country is impoverished by military operations it is due to distant transportation; carriage of supplies for great distances renders the people destitute.'* As a superb logistician, Sun reminds his readers that to deliver a single bushel (8 gallons dry weight) of supplies to troops fighting in enemy territory consumes twenty bushels.

Sun's words are as true today as when written, his works are still studied in army staff colleges worldwide. The art of keeping an army in the field and providing it with the means to impose the will of its political masters has never changed. The British Expeditionary Force (BEF) that fought on the Western Front in the years 1914-1918 developed a system of motorised transport (MT) that excelled and became a vitally important contributor to victory. An army on campaign that neglects logistics will be inviting defeat, as demonstrated below.

The works of Sun Tzu were published in Paris in 1792, Bonaparte was said to have been an avid reader. However, neither Bonaparte nor Adolf Hitler appear to have taken heed of the wisdom of Sun Tzu. Had they done so, it would have been obvious that to mount a successful attack into the terrifying vastness of Russia would require an enormously long and secure supply chain that could operate in all weathers, the Russian winter not being a recent invention even in the year 1812 when the French Army attempted to 'march out' of Russia.

Bonaparte's usual feeding methods involved his armies foraging on either side of his line of march. His 600,000 (estimates vary) soldiers needed 3,500 calories per man per day to keep them fit for fighting and marching, as almost the only means the troops had of covering the 600 miles to Moscow was to walk. Should Bonaparte's plan have succeeded, the newly conquered Russians would have been expected to feed the invaders. Due to the lack of roads in Russia, Bonaparte's army had to advance in a long single column instead of several parallel columns. This led to those in the ranks nearer to the front having first choice of the food gathered, those further to the rear found little or nothing to eat. The Russians refused to fight a series of pitched battles except at Borodino and, combined with the Russian policy of 'scorched earth', the French were soon in serious difficulties as they advanced into a barren and unforgiving trap. Moscow proved to be empty of food, leaving no option for the French but retreat. Worse was to come as they retreated in a land where all available food had been either destroyed or confiscated by the Russians. 'General Winter' also joined battle on the side of Mother Russia, with incessant blizzards and temperatures that fell below -30C. Bonaparte's over reaching of his logistic capability resulted in the loss of 480,000 men. Horse power was the only means of moving supplies and with the animals dying in huge numbers, the transport system collapsed. The horses had not even been equipped with 'winter' shoes which would have allowed them to grip the snow and ice encountered during the retreat. How many of the 250,000 horses that set out upon this ill-starred folly ever returned home is not known.

As for Hitler, he relied upon wildly inaccurate forecasts of swift and easy victory. The railways were the prime movers of very large loads of vital supplies but the Russian railways did not run on 'Standard Gauge' so German locomotives could not cross the border until a phenomenal amount of remedial work had been completed. Some 80-90 per cent of German army transport was horse drawn; the largely conscripted lorry fleet proved unreliable and even handcarts were pressed into service. Logistic failure ensued, leading to many thousands of German soldiers freezing to death because at the start of the campaign in June they had only been issued with summer clothing. Without the means of getting enough food forward to the troops, thousands more starved to death along with the poor, luckless horses who shared their fate, trapped in the bleak hopelessness of the endless frozen wastes of Russia. On the vital role of logistics, Churchill proclaimed:

> *Victory is the beautiful bright coloured flower, transport is the stem without which it could never have blossomed. If money is the sinew of war, transport and supply are its arteries.*

It is a historical fact that the most successful military commanders were natural logisticians, or, they were lucky enough to have trusted staff officers who fulfilled that role.

In this work there is much about the 'other ranks' and the junior officers who together shouldered the burden of the early years of MT and in so doing, became modern logisticians who would not be out of place today. Mention should also be made of an ASC driver who had served in the Great War; the author briefly made his acquaintance over forty years ago when the old pioneer was a bus passenger. He always wore his long ASC-type coat with boots and gaiters and made an imposing figure, tall with a mane of swept back silver hair. While waiting for departure time the old soldier would drop out morsels regarding driving lorries in France 1914-18. Like thousands of others, upon his return to civilian life he used his new driving skills in the frantic scramble for work that followed the end of the war. One of his favourite stories was of the long running rivalry between motor vehicle drivers and their opposite numbers who drove steam traction engines. These engines were powerful but slow, often pulling two or three trailers; they would not pull over for a 'motor man' instead they would 'put the blower on' that is to send a jet of steam up the engine's chimney to draw the fire. A side effect of this action was to send showers of sparks over following vehicles. 'They tried to set yer afire,' was how the old ASC man described this forthright show of contempt.

This work is a humble offering to the memory of all those pioneers of MT who conquered fear and drove through shell and bullet fire and never let the infantry down. Should their spirits still roam the now quiet lanes of France and Flanders, may they roam therefore in peace.

Un-named ASC Corporal and lorry, late 1917.

Chapter 1

Street Hygiene and Traffic Congestion

Even prior to the rise of the motor omnibus, Sir Edward Knight declared in 1906 that: *'The use of motors would save 25% of the space on London's roads and, therefore solve the problem of approaching traffic paralysis.'*

Sir Edward was also an enthusiast for bus lanes and one-way streets; his ideas also included 'smokeless zones' for no other reason than to *'get the coal traffic off the streets'*. Photographic evidence from the early twentieth century, reveal a city grinding to a halt; how drivers managed to negotiate the completely blocked road junctions must remain a mystery. The mass use of horses in a city environment posed a serious threat to the health of the inhabitants. London, as the largest city in the world in the early twentieth century, had an enormous problem with the waste produced by the natural bodily processes of horses on the city's streets. A horse will produce between 15 and 35 pounds of solid waste per day. With 40,000 'bussers' and 11,000 cab horses, plus an untold number of 'vanners' and general trade horses, the amount of waste on the streets reached staggering proportions.

The waste in its turn attracted legions of flies only too eager to come to the feast, leading to the spread of typhoid fever together with numerous other diseases. The problem became so acute that in the year 1894 it became known as the 'Great Stink', *The Times* declaring that: *'In 50 years, every street in London will be buried under nine feet of manure.'*

For many, the coming of the motor vehicle offered salvation for the large towns and cities. In the countryside, it became noticeable that cattle would congregate in places near a road used by motors; it was quickly realised that exhaust smoke drove away the otherwise relentless flies that mercilessly attacked the long-suffering cattle.

This writer spent his 1950s childhood in a street served by three horses and can still recall the smell of manure. As the manure dried out and was crushed by the wheels of passing vehicles, a gust of wind would raise clouds of noxious material. Enthusiastic gardeners living in the street would collect some, but never all, of the waste; imagine then, the sheer size of the problem confronting London. The image depicts Armoury Road, a cul-de-sac in Birmingham, where he spent his childhood. This appears to be an early post Second Word War photo, the gap in the houses on the left was due to bomb damage that occurred when the Birmingham Small Arms factory situated on the opposite side of the road, was targeted by Germany with great loss of life to the workers in the factory. Note the tailboard on the milk float, a favourite target for 'us kids' to catch a free ride.

General Staffs worldwide, worked on possible confrontations, alliances, military and naval responses, to a variety of situations that

Horse drawn milk float, Armoury Rd. Birmingham, source unknown.

could develop if the art of diplomacy failed. In the early twentieth century, the British General Staff, realising that the vital supply of horses was showing signs of dwindling, developed plans to increase MT within the British Army. It must be stressed that horse transport did not disappear from the BEF – as of 31 August 1917, 449,880 horses and mules were hard at work on the supply lines. The main reason for the retention of these wonderful animals was their ability to work 'off road'; where rails and usable roads ended the horses took over. Despite their often being portrayed as such, horses and mules *did not* go up to the front lines. As an example of 'horse sense', in a dire emergency when a massive enemy bombardment struck the Caterpillar Valley on the Somme, endangering the hundreds of horses kept there, the order was given to cut the tethers and let them run free. The horses immediately turned away from the front and disappeared in the opposite direction as hard as they could go.

Due to prolonged association, horses often became pets; in war situations when men and animals shared the same risks of death, the wounding or violent death of his horse could seriously affect the soldier. Charles Lander mentions in *Lander's War* (Tommies' Guides 2010) he was near Mametz Wood on the Somme when he was approached by an artilleryman who asked Lander to despatch his very badly wounded horse. Lander could not bring himself to do as requested and told the man to carry on till he found a qualified person. Moments later Lander observed a Royal Artillery officer who promptly shot the poor horse through the head.

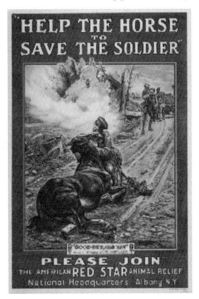

Vanners, Bussers, Jibbers and Wheelers

To trace the rise of MT in the British Army it is worthwhile looking as far back as the early 1900s. Officers charged with the supply of horses to the army noticed that the number of fit horses for sale, or those that could

Evocative poster by the prolific artist, Fortunino Matania, 1881-1963.

be retained under the subsidy scheme, had begun to decline. Added to which, the costs of the overall care for the animals was rising to the point that the first year's cost of care was equalling the original purchase price of the horse. Writing in 1912, a journalist employed by a motor magazine (unbiased?) claimed that the cost of a van horse ('vanner') complete with van was £90 (£3,875 today) as opposed to £380 (£16,362) for a motor van, more than four times as expensive. Against these large price differences, the case for the motor van was argued by its ready availability seven days per week as opposed to the 'vanner' who worked a five-day week and only 45-50 hours at work. Also, it was claimed that a horse could not become a 'vanner' until it was six years old and then work for a maximum of seven years. Although not mentioned by the above journalist, at the end of the horse's working day, for that of its owner it was not, he or she still had work to do to keep the horse fit and active; grooming and inspection of the animal was vital plus all the 'tack' had to be kept clean and oiled to prevent sores developing. At the same time, supplying horses for the Territorial Army was becoming increasingly difficult; persuading an owner to part with a horse for two evenings per week and a Saturday was not conducive to the running of a business even allowing for payment of a subsidy.

An independent 'Vanner'?

A short tale of a 'vanner' who worked in the inner-city area of Birmingham was told to the writer by an old friend of many years standing. The horse in question worked on a baker's van and knew the round as well, if not better, than the human two-man team that he or she worked with. The driver and his mate served many terraced houses and back-to-backs that were situated at right angles to the main streets which in effect meant that horse and van were out of sight. All was usually routine when the men returned to the van, the horse would move on to the next stopping point without a word from the crew. But life being what it is, the day dawned when the men returned to find that the horse and van were nowhere to be seen. A prolonged search of the surrounding streets proved fruitless leaving the now 'horseless' pair no option but to return to the depot and explain themselves.

A walk of forty minutes duration ensued with ever rising levels of apprehension; how to account for loss of the horse, van and the payload of bread? They need not have worried, the first sight that greeted them in the depot yard was their much-loved horse complete with van and load. The horse was calmly munching on a good feed without a care in the world, having negotiated the traffic and road junctions of inner-city Birmingham. After much leg pulling and scratching of heads by those deemed the most knowledgeable in equine matters, it was concluded that someone or something had frightened the horse who promptly declared independence and headed for home.

The 'Busser' or the London omnibus horse

A meeting held in London in 1912 was informed that over a period of three years, the London 'busser' had almost disappeared from the city's streets due to the rapid uptake of the motor bus by the passenger transport companies. Twelve horses were required to keep a bus in service with a team of two; each pair worked for three hours. There were 40,000 'bussers' at work in London around the year 1910. The 'busser' was well known for its ability to take the role of artillery horse during training and annual camps with the Territorial Army. The usual place in the gun team for a 'busser' was that of 'wheeler', that is nearest to the gun where their fitness and bodily strength were used as the main means of braking. However, by 1912, finding horse 'busser' teams proved very difficult and was predicted to become more so in the years to come.

To overcome shortages at the annual camps, horses were hired in at the rate of £5 (£215) per fortnight camp. The old term 'horse trading' springs to mind with frequent reports of totally unfit horses being provided, whether due to age, illness or in many cases being a 'jibber', that is a horse who refused point blank to work. On the rare occasion of getting the 'jibber' into harness at all, the result would be commotion as the horse would not co-operate, not even when the other equine members of the team tried to set a good example.

The Case of two Jibbers

Picture the scene as witnessed by the writer; it is the late twentieth century, a Sunday morning in the yard of an old Warwickshire public house known as The Case Is Altered. A horse bus pulled by two large 'bussers' enters the pub yard and the passengers alight to sample the wares on offer. The horses meanwhile are the real centre of attention as all and sundry make a fuss of them. Fed, watered and fussed over, the horses nuzzle their many admirers. Departure time arrived with all the passengers and crew safely on board. Now was the time when matters began to unravel; our equine friends refused to move and no amount of cajoling or encouragement had the slightest effect, the bus remained stationary. Just prior to the writer leaving, eight people, two to each wheel, at the command 'go' heaved on the spokes, but all to no avail. The horses took not the slightest notice, in effect, 'we are in charge and you lot can await our pleasure'. Or, a case of two 'bussers' who opted to become 'jibbers'?

Horses and the Economy of the UK

Prior to the First World War, horses were a very large means of employment, about 85 per cent of the country's goods were carried at some time by horse drawn vehicles. At a lecture given in 1912, by Colonel H.H. Mulliner, entitled 'The Supply of Horses for the Territorial Force', a Mr H. Baxendale declared:

> *It would produce lamentable results to seize a great number of horses if war was declared, as a very large number of people would be thrown out of employment. A trade horse practically carried three people in work.*

In reply, the chairman, Colonel J.E.B. Seeley, reminded Mr Baxendale and the audience that:

> *In the event of war and mobilisation, the War Office was to see that the greatest care would be taken that no undue hardship was caused to owners when horses would be taken on mobilisation. The full value of the horse would be paid by the War Office. It is impossible for any country to keep enough horses to satisfy demand in war; therefore, the State must take them, and pay for them when the emergency arises.*

As an example of the scale and cost of horse transport before the First World War, John Sumner, a Birmingham grocer who went on to establish the Typhoo Tea Company, kept twenty 'vanners' at 30s (shillings) per horse, per week, for feeding, grooming and stabling, equal in 2015 values to £86 per week per horse, totalling £1,720 for all twenty.

Although this work primarily concerns the rise of MT, it is only fair to the horses that we remind ourselves that horse power still had many years of useful service ahead; as previously mentioned, horses were by far the mainstay of the German Army's transport in the Second World War. In Great Britain, horses still outnumbered tractors in agricultural work as late as 1939. A valid reason for the retention of horses was their innate intelligence. Another example of clever horses were those that hauled the City of Birmingham Refuse Department narrow boats as late as 1964. To witness the horses working the Camp Hill flight of locks on the Grand Union Canal without a word of command was amazing.

A glorious story told by the narrow boat crews concerned one of their favourite horses, who when the dinner time stop (it was never lunch) was made and the horse was unharnessed, would gallop off into the distance. The crews soon learned to give up the chase as the horse always returned exactly on time to start work. The last 'vanner' noted by the writer worked on a milk round until the early 1970s in the village of Knowle, Warwickshire.

Chapter 2

Tentative Beginnings for MT

Trials and Tribulations

From the time of Cromwell, the British Army had been viewed with suspicion by those who occupied seats in parliament and were charged with the defence of the realm. Following the wars from the Civil War to the South African War, when hostilities ceased the Army was reduced as soon as possible and deprived of funds for development, thereby, in the view of the politicians, the Army could not be used against its own masters. It was against this background of parsimony and outright suspicion that from the year 1904 onwards, the military began to experiment with machines that could replace the horse, save money and increase mobility. The dilemma facing the Army at this time was the high initial purchase price of motor transport (MT), while at the same time there were huge numbers of horses which still had to be cared for.

The mighty power of steam had been available for some time. Steam tractors and waggons were powerful and reliable machines, however, they needed a plentiful and reliable source of clean water to constantly replenish the ever-thirsty boiler in order to produce steam for the motive power. Driver training was also more involved as lack of attention to the boiler, especially in a battle situation, could prove catastrophic with the possibility of explosion. Shell splinters striking the boiler would cause an instantaneous burst, most likely ending in the death by scalding of the driver and fireman. The steam powered vehicles were also much heavier than the petrol motor lorry and more expensive to produce. For these reasons, the War Office opted for the motor lorry to fulfil its road transport needs, although some steam tractors did work on the Western Front throughout the war but usually well away from the range of the enemy's artillery. The Birmingham firm of Belliss & Morcom were still supplying

Experimental Thornycroft steam waggon. (Courtesy of R. Pullen)

stationary steam engines in the early 1970s to parts of the world that had plenty of wood and water but little or no coal or oil reserves.

One of the advantageous features of MT was the higher thermal efficiency of the Internal Combustion Engine (ICE), that is the fuel converted into energy inside the engine via a spark ignition which 'explodes' the fuel. Steam engines burn the fuel outside the working parts of the engine, losing a part of the heat energy before it can be applied. For many years, ICEs were known as 'exploders'; the vast majority of MT used by the British Army was of the petrol-fuelled type. The sale of petrol (officially, petroleum spirit) to the public had only come about a few years prior to the First World War. Governments were concerned that disasters would occur if petrol was handled by people with no experience of the volatility of the liquid. Petrol was often delivered to car owners' houses in containers of glass or metal, thereby providing endless opportunities for fire or explosion.

When funds permitted, various schemes had been tried to evaluate MT with varying degrees of success leading to a hard-hitting lecture entitled '*The Organisation of Power Traction on the Roads for National Defence*' given in 1907 by Colonel Sir John Macdonald. He forcefully described the lack of preparedness of the country's land defences and the acute shortage of motor transport. Macdonald, a member of the Royal Motor Reserve, castigated the government for continually depriving the home army of funds, while at the same time assuring the public that all was well with the nation's defences. Militarism was on the rise in Europe and large raids or even full-scale invasion along Britain's east coast was deemed a strong possibility. Should those of ill intent succeed in avoiding the attentions of the Royal Navy and set about their depredations, then how to counter and ultimately eject the wrongdoers taxed the brains of many a strategist, both professional and 'armchair'.

That the railways at the time (110 years ago) were prime movers of people and goods cannot be denied, though what railways have always suffered from is lack of flexibility; in most cases goods require onward despatch from the station they are consigned to, usually by motor vehicle. (Although, in these troubled times of road congestion such a system may have merit.) Should a hostile landing take place requiring a mass, rapid deployment of troops, stores and ammunition, over many miles of thinly populated coast threatened by invasion, the railway could not fulfil this desperate requirement. Trains on the East Coast or West Coast lines could carry troops and make stops in isolated locations where the soldiers would have to jump down onto the tracks to de-train. This was a high-risk action, more so in heavy rain and darkness; the railway signalling system would also be compromised by halting the train as described above and could easily trigger the 'six bells' signal meaning Obstruction Danger. At this, all signals must show a red aspect and all traffic be brought to a standstill; it could not be re-started until a responsible official had made absolutely certain that the tracks were safe before signing a form to that effect.

Also mentioned was the difficulty that 'fast, urgent' trains would encounter when attempting to overtake a slower train; this was only possible when a suitable siding of the correct length was available to accommodate the slow train. Unloading the Army's stores and equipment on isolated stretches of track would have involved herculean labour as the floor of a goods waggon is approximately level with the shoulders of a 6ft-tall man who would be standing on the ground at the edge of the track ballasting. In the matter of the vitally important field artillery, the weight of the guns would have precluded any attempts at trackside unloading. The 18pdr gun weighed about 1¼ tons, plus the weight of the ammunition and, without its six-horse team, the gun was immobilised.

With the railways choked with traffic from both north and south and facing the very real possibility that the enemy would, in order to paralyse troop movements, have destroyed as much of the track system as he could, how would the vast numbers of troops be concentrated in order to begin the task of bringing the invaders to battle?

Marching would be the age-old answer. The *Field Service Pocket Book* issued to officers in 1914 advises that marching troops average 3 miles per hour. How far can a soldier realistically be expected to march? Perhaps 25 miles on the first day, thereafter the efficiency of the troops would diminish further and faster following each day's march. Marching records were broken during the BEF's 1914 retreat from Mons, but for the most part the troops were in no condition to fight while averaging 15 miles per day for the 200-mile retreat. The line of retreat was littered with kit that the soldiers had discarded in desperate attempts to lighten their loads. A part of the BEF stood and fought on 25 August at Le Cateau, continuing the retreat the next day and always covered by a cavalry screen. A march from Aldershot to Kingston-upon-Hull would entail 222 miles of forced march taking approximately fifteen days with, most probably, a result as detailed above. Would horse power have provided the answer to worn out marching troops? The answer must be no; there were never anything like sufficient numbers of carts and horse buses to save the legs of 250,000 men plus their daily supplies of food, water and ammunition, not forgetting the huge amounts of fodder required to feed the horses.

We must also bear in mind that a horse is no different from a human being in that its physical endurance falls quickly away when not fed and properly rested. The Army was not indifferent to the welfare of horses as the *Field Service Pocket Book* is quite specific regarding feeding, watering and resting the horses. The book reminds its reader that horses do not drink well in the early morning, so a stop for water should be made following three hours on the road. Following a drink, the horse was not to be pushed hard as this could cause severe problems. Food should always be given before water, never after. And, most importantly, the horse should be allowed a minimum of five hours in twenty-four to properly digest food and drink. In a war situation large bodies of cavalry would be advancing or retreating with little or no time to observe the finer points of animal welfare; this is not to decry the authors of *Field Service Regulations,* they were duty-bound to insist on the highest possible standards available at any one time.

Cavalry, a weapons system in which the horse was a key component, was used either in the role of mounted infantry or in the traditional role of the charge to deliver 'shock and awe' to the enemy. The writer can testify to the shock and panic that ensues when confronted with a charging horse. When walking up an avenue of trees during a visit to the Somme village of Mailly-Maillet a commotion broke out ahead with shouts of alarm; the writer and friends soon discovered the cause of the alarm as a bolting horse came into view leaving no alternative but to dive for cover, the ground vibrating as the horse thundered past. We later discovered that the indiscriminate use of a car horn had frightened the horse which had been quietly standing with its owner who was dismounted and holding the reins. A fit cavalry horse could gallop at 15 mph but, unlike those taking part in old 'Wild West' films where horse and rider gallop from horizon to horizon, the gallop could only be maintained for short distances, the usual on-the-road speed being 3½ mph.

So, what could commanders expect of these new-fangled motor vehicles? On good roads a continuous 10 mph was easily achieved with the added advantage that the motor would keep going as long as it was supplied with fuel and a driver. Could this be the answer to the conundrum facing those charged with the responsibility of repelling a raid or full-scale invasion? Colonel Macdonald quoted figures in 1907 for the increasing number of motor vehicles in Great Britain which had reached 120,000 and was rising by 500 per week, being supplied by domestic manufacturers plus many more by American and French makers. The colonel then related to his audience an epic journey recently undertaken by himself and his son:

> *A few months ago, I had to drive a car weighing a ton and a half from Coventry to Edinburgh, a distance of 326 miles, and circumstances made it necessary that I should be only two days on the journey. My son and I – driving alternately –*

*reached Carlisle in time for dinner on the first day, driving
through the busy streets of Warrington, Wigan and Preston,
and the narrow streets of Lancaster and Kendal, and lastly in
the dark over Shap summit and through Penrith, covering in
all 223 miles. On the second day we arrived in Edinburgh –
103 miles –before two-o-clock in the afternoon. It must be plain
to everyone what could be accomplished in an emergency by
such vehicles.*

An example of the need for extreme caution in the headlong rush to
adopt the new technology tragically occurred in 1906, but not mentioned
by Colonel Macdonald in his 1907 lecture. A Vanguard Company bus
carrying thirty-four passengers in July 1906, came off the London to
Brighton road at Hand Cross Hill. Ten people were killed and twenty-
two injured when the bus collided with an oak tree which virtually
severed the upper deck from the lower.

Several facets of the accident combined to cause the disaster.
The driver was unfamiliar with the road which, unlike today, did
not have a tarmac surface and the hill was a steep descent with tight
bends and an adverse camber. Witnesses claimed that the bus had
gathered speed when the driver attempted to change to a lower gear
to use the engine as a brake. As he did so, part of the transmission
disintegrated casting pieces of metal into the road. The normal brakes
were unable to hold the bus and nothing could stop the centrifugal
force generated by the vehicle's speed, the right-hand bend and the
adverse camber; disaster was the inevitable consequence of a series
of errors. The present writer can testify that in 1970, bus drivers
using crash gear boxes, were instructed in no uncertain terms to
*'change down as soon as you see the steep hill sign, not when you
think about it later'.*

At the time of Colonel Macdonald's lecture in February 1907 there
were already 1,000 motor 'omnibuses' operating quite successfully in
London, with an extra thousand to come into service by the end of
the year: omnibus being the key word, a bus that can go anywhere.
The colonel calculated that if, in a national emergency, the London
General Omnibus Company, could be persuaded to part with 1,500 of
its vehicles complete with drivers, 45,000 troops could be transported
180 miles in one day. It should be borne in mind that there was no

real experience of such large movements. Petrol, oil and lubricants would have to be stockpiled and relief drivers provided together with mechanics to accomplish the inevitable repairs. Much would still need to be done to avert the danger of the Home Army being unable to respond to invasion in a controlled concentration powerful enough to deter the most aggressive potential invader.

The Early Trials

The Lancashire Heavy Motor Vehicle Trials took place between 1898 and 1901. These trials tested motors over 30-40-mile courses which included hill-climbs and tests of manoeuvrability. The soon to be famous names of Thornycroft and Leyland appeared in the 1898 trial in which both firms submitted steam-powered vehicles, the Leyland winning the first prize of £100 (£7,817). For the 1901 trial, two petrol-driven vehicles were entered plus eight steam-powered types. The War Office were on hand to witness the trial, taking a keen interest.

It was the good fortune of the War Office that private operators were the real pioneers of MT. It was they who, at their own expense, experimented and improved designs from hard won experience gained on the highways and byways of Great Britain. A major contributor to the knowledge of motor bus operation was the Worthing Motor Omnibus Company who, via failed trials with steam power, purchased a Milnes-Daimler saloon (single deck) motor bus in 1904 to run a short but, regular service between Tarring and East Worthing at 15-minute intervals; a service was later established between Worthing and Brighton which still runs to this day. These services were beset with mechanical problems leading to bankruptcies. It was to be 1909 before yet another company (Worthing Motor Services) would be formed and crowned with operational success. The resumed Brighton service proved very popular with both residents and visitors. So, free of charge the government, through the trials and tribulations of others, gained a very large fund of knowledge that soon became available to the military.

The 1908 trials were a serious attempt to quantify the usefulness of MT. This was at a time when its reliability became an important issue if the government was to spend large amounts of taxpayer's money converting to motor vehicles. Only the year before the trials in 1907 the Birmingham and Midland Motor Omnibus company (Midland Red) had forsaken motor buses due to reliability problems and reverted to the more trustworthy horse. The company did not re-equip with motor buses until 1912 by which time many of the earlier problems of reliability had been solved. The directors of Midland Red were correct to be concerned given the tragic events at Hand Cross Hill which would not have gone unnoticed by the military. For the purposes of the trial it was supposed that a hostile landing had taken place on the Essex coast. The nearest body of troops large enough to expel the invaders were based at Brentwood. The trial was to explore the possibility of carrying troops by bus and so have them arrive in a fit condition to fight the invader before he could push forward inland.

As reported by Lieutenant General Paget of Eastern Command, the motor bus was showing promise as a quick and efficient means

London buses and lorries off to war.

of transporting troops. It was found that up to thirty troops could be carried at an average speed of 12 mph over a good road surface and in favourable weather, otherwise the speed would drop to 9-10 mph. The men's equipment and stores were carried in separate buses. By having the men and stores properly arranged, it was noted that a whole battalion of 1,000 troops could be loaded and ready to depart in five or ten minutes. The potential value of the bus in the evacuation of the wounded was also noted in that, the vehicle would not require much, if any, modification, was speedy and well sprung and could travel considerable distances to a place of safety.

The year 1909 saw the introduction of a new weight limit set by the Metropolitan Police, whereby the unladen weight of a bus was not to exceed 3.5 tons. Perhaps inadvertently, this regulation gave rise to more efficient vehicles – the world-famous Daimler 'B' Type and the less well-known KPL (Knight-Pieper-Lanchester).

The latter, a petrol-electric vehicle of very advanced design and of monocoque (without the use of a heavy chassis) construction and an all-metal body, was very strong and at the same time lightweight. The bus was of four-wheel drive layout, each wheel being driven by a separate electric motor which, when tractive effort was not required, became dynamos sending energy to storage batteries. The petrol engine was fitted with the luxury of an electric starter

Well established London motor buses, 1914.

instead of the widely used starting handle (well known for breaking the driver's wrist). At prolonged stops or termini the engine could be stopped, saving fuel and preventing fumes and noise on the city streets. However, the KPL did not find favour with omnibus operators; Midland Red trialled one example on its Hagley Road services in 1910, before returning the bus without placing an order. The KPL was also subjected to intensive trials in London by technical advisors working for the Chief Commissioner of Police but unfortunately for all those involved with the KPL, no orders were placed. Much of the KPL design has now found favour in the twenty-first century – perhaps in 1910, it was just too advanced? Frederick Lanchester was a London-born polymath responsible for many automotive inventions who spent most of his working life in Birmingham. He died at his home 'Dyott End', in Oxford Road, Birmingham in 1946.

The petrol-electric drive did come into use mainly by the Tilling-Stevens company. They were popular because horse bus drivers often found great difficulty in mastering the constant mesh (crash type) gear boxes of conventional buses and lorries. Crash gearboxes required two clutch depressions, the use of the ear to detect the correct engine revolutions and perfect timing when shifting the gear lever. A failure to comply with any one of the requirements would bring forth embarrassing crunching and grinding noises from the gear box and worse still, missing a gear which could cause a stall going uphill or loss of engine braking downhill. The Midland Red operated crash box buses as late as the mid-1970s, there being far less to go wrong than with the more modern and easier on the leg and knee, synchromesh gear boxes.

In 1910 the Daimler 'B' Type was introduced to the streets of the capital; here at last was a simple but reliable omnibus fitted with an excellent 40 horse power (HP) engine. Born of operational experience, many 'B' Types were to find themselves serving on the Western Front, from where, with luck, a lot were to return to London and gave long periods of reliable service. That year also

Frederick W. Lanchester, engineering genius.

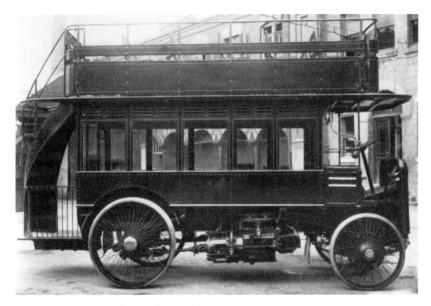

Knight-Pieper-Lanchester (KPL) bus.

witnessed the amalgamation of Daimler with the Birmingham Small Arms Company (BSA). The new organisation went on to play a vital role in arms and vehicle production in the coming war.

By 1911 the pace of MT expansion in the UK business market was increasing rapidly. A lecture given that year mentions the acquisition by the War Office of the 20-ton 'Lion' and the 6-ton 'Foster' steam tractors and of great significance, *'the really up to date system of traction, the petrol motor lorry'*. Already, those proponents of MT were observing the London motor buses and their ever-increasing numbers and reliability. Could the bus be designed in such a way as to make it possible *'by removing a few bolts'* to exchange the bus body for that of a lorry? This proved to be the case; the bus bodies of the time were those used by horse buses and, coupled with the jolting caused by cobbled streets and the solid tyres of the vehicle, the body required easy removal to facilitate the frequent overhauls needed as components broke or worked loose.

Money, and how to obtain the new vehicles? The Royal Navy, the Senior Service, always had first call on funds, as the protection of Great Britain's oceanic lifelines was vital, together with the need to deter any hostile nation from causing mischief. The Army had to take what funds were left and do the best it could. However, it was noted that some ship owners were receiving subsidies from government on the understanding that, in the event of war, their vessels would come under Admiralty control. Could not this system be applied to owners of motor vehicles?

The matter was quickly resolved as in the same year of 1911, the Secretary of State for War, Richard Haldane, realising the fast-moving changes in MT could no longer be ignored, introduced an annual subsidy for motor vehicles that

Lord Haldane, Minister for War.

would allow use of the vehicles for training purposes and surrender to the War Office should a war require their use.

Whether a bus, lorry or van is to be used, they all need a competent driver, without which they are nothing more than expensive liabilities. Motor vehicle driving skills were not at all widespread in 1911 leading once more to the London omnibus companies being caught in the 'headlights' of those seeking a solution. It should be mentioned that an unofficial proposal was put forward prior to the announcement of the subsidy scheme, to recruit the most experienced drivers for buses to be used in war, notably, the London bus drivers into the Army Service Corps Reserve at the rate of a shilling per day above their company wages. It was also proposed to confidentially install an officer in the companies who would observe and record the working practices involved to keep a busy fleet running on the streets of London. The drivers would not be exempt from observation of their 'character and disposition'. A glance at the rule book of the Midland Red would have reassured the 'embedded' officer: Rule 3 declares: '*All Drivers and Conductors shall work in harmony with all other servants of the Company and shall be of strictly temperate habits.*'

It was now that officers began to realise that the lorry as well as the motor bus would become vital components of any expeditionary force despatched overseas in the event of a European war. Tests had shown that fifty men could be crowded on to a lorry to dash to threatened areas or, concentrate for a major attack. The 'B' Type bus proved its worth in this respect as the previously mentioned trials had shown the ease of conversion from bus to lorry; a flexible transport system that would be the envy of fleet managers today. Much work had yet to be done to standardise the new 'subsidy' vehicles. Two classes were stipulated: the Class A (3 ton) and the Class B (30 cwt) or (1½ ton) lorry. Buses were included in the latter as the gearing, although very good for stop and start work on busy streets, proved in trials to be slow and prone to overheating on hilly roads when carrying a 3-ton load. When used on Class B work the 'B' Type proved to be very reliable.

Subsidy lorries were expected to climb hills of 1 in 8 when fully loaded and travel at walking pace without stalling the engine. This sounds simple to us as our vehicles adjust themselves to different driving conditions. Up to the late 1930s, drivers of motor vehicles had to adjust the engine's ignition system by hand via a lever often located on the steering column. This was known as 'Advance and Retard' – get it wrong and pops and bangs would emanate from the engine, overheating or, stalling would follow. Therefore, to successfully climb a hill or cope with bumper to bumper low speeds, the driver had to develop a skill to keep the engine running at optimum efficiency. Life could become even more complicated. Troubles on the road included the petrol tap turning itself off thereby bringing the vehicle to an abrupt halt or, stopping following loud spluttering from the engine. This was usually caused by water being present in the fuel, an unhappy condition which generally came about by *'carelessness in filling up!'*

We tend to think of the multi-fuel engine as a product of our time, but surprisingly, 'subsidy' vehicles were expected to run on three different types of fuel: petrol, alcohol and Benzole. Petrol and alcohol need no explanation, but for the benefit of younger readers, Benzole was one of the some 200 by-products of coal. Benzole contained toluene, itself a volatile substance which can strip paint and also has explosive properties that were used during the First World War. Running a vehicle on Benzole used to be seen as patriotic as the coal shale from which it was produced was mined in the UK and therefore not dependent on expensive imports. Benzole disappeared from garages during the late 1960s.

Having overcome all the difficulties of purchasing a motor vehicle, gained some idea of the rudiments of driving the machine (driving tests were in the far distant future), a venture forth onto the 'High Toby' would be eagerly anticipated. But, although the highways outside cities were called roads, most were nothing but narrow lanes surfaced with stone and dust which would be sprayed with water to form

The famous 'National' petrol logo.

a rather dubious 'adhesive' surface. This was fine for pedestrian and horse traffic, not so with the new motor vehicles which broke through the thin surface and in dry weather, raised clouds of white dust up to 20ft high which followed the vehicle for its entire journey. It is easy to see why drivers of motors became very unpopular very quickly. Should the weather in the UK be wet, a not uncommon occurrence, jets of mud and liquefied dust would be splashed over any unfortunate pedestrians within range. The would-be driver would also discover that horses hated the new motor vehicles and there were instances where the horse rider/ driver raised the whip to the passing motorist.

Nagging doubts continued for the Army regarding multiple makes and types of MT that might be pressed into service for war; the supply of spare parts for many different makes was quite rightly seen as a potential cause of chaos. To overcome the spare parts problem, it was mooted that the government should purchase all the lorries needed for war and run them as a nation-wide haulage company in peacetime to cover the costs. It was a not so far-fetched an idea. Older readers may remember British Road Services which came into being after the Second World War, now long since faded into history.

The year 1912 arrived along with more experience gained with MT. In particular, drivers were now ordered to stop and engage low gear before attempting to descend a hill. With the Hand Cross Hill fatal crash in mind, this was and still is a wise precaution, especially with a crash box in inexperienced hands. Practice showed that 30 yards should be allowed between buses when large bodies of troops were involved, noting that telegraph poles were 60 yards apart, the poles served as ready-made stop markers (bus stops) to allow troops to board. In trials of that year, lorries achieved a run of 50 miles with troops plus food and equipment; this was the equivalent of two days of the most extreme form of forced marching. The future was the motor.

The horse had his enemies and as he couldn't write he could not reply to remarks such as: *The horse is still to be used where he can be shot at; as to those recently seen in a camp, it would be kinder to dispose of them now; they would disgrace an old cab horse.* Well thankfully, we know that 'Old Dobbin' outlived all of his detractors!

In 1913, one year before the world would be changed forever by war, diplomatic relations with the German Empire were deteriorating. Although not bound by treaty, Great Britain had been in talks with France for some years to come to her aid in the event of an invasion by Germany. Russia had also formed an alliance with France as she feared German expansion eastwards into Russian-held spheres of influence.

This year also saw the emergence of some standardisation in vehicles involved in the government 'subsidy' scheme. It was recognised quite early that MT could not operate 'off road', the horse would still shoulder the burden of cross-country work. Solid rubber tyres became standard as opposed to wheel rims made from steel as used on horse-drawn waggons. The layout of the foot pedals became the same as those used to this day, although the writer once owned a 1934 Morris Cowley in which the accelerator was positioned between the clutch and the foot brake. The gear and hand brake levers had to be of different lengths, the gear lever being fitted with the distinctive ball-shaped head that we know so well. The vehicles of both A and B classes were expected to safely ascend and descend 1 in 6 hills compared with the 1 in 8 of previous years. The petrol tank actually served as the driver's seat and held 30 gallons of petrol, enough to accomplish a run of 200 miles. The tanks were fitted with a visual indicator and the driver would be held responsible if he ran out of petrol.

The engines were fitted with governors limiting the engine to 1,000 rpm (revolutions per minute), by so doing over revving of the engine was avoided, as were the dangers of 'passing and repassing' when in convoy. Maximum speeds of the two classes were stipulated at, class A at 16 mph and class B at 20 mph. A fitting of 'sprags' was also deemed necessary; these trailed behind the vehicle which, if stalled or the driver missed a gear when ascending a hill, the sprag would dig into the soft surface of the road and prevent a backwards runaway. The minimum ground clearance allowed was 12 inches – '*more if possible*' – to allow for the rutted road surfaces likely to be encountered in a war zone. This still holds good today with military lorries. The interchange of spare parts had also improved but still much more was needed, the all-important magneto being specifically required to conform to quick change methods.

By late 1913, the London General Omnibus Company was running a fleet of 2,194 'B' Type buses and between May and November of that year the vehicles covered the amazing distance of 55,065,235 miles. Approximately 0.120 per cent of that mileage was 'lost' mainly due to traffic congestion and street accidents.

There were backward slips in MT reliability, often caused by bad design and/or poor maintenance. On one occasion a short run to the seaside involved so many breakdowns that the passengers were forced to travel home by train, but not before they had spent the whole night in a station waiting room. On the side of excellent results, in 1914 a Dennis charabanc (car with seats) on a 660-mile holiday trip between Eastbourne and Lands End, behaved perfectly and arrived back in Eastbourne exactly on time. Many of the twenty-three passengers immediately booked in advance for another holiday by the same means.

Almost on the eve of war, in the then tranquil village of Knowle in Warwickshire, the senior members of the church choir had just '*spent an enjoyable day in a new way, a Cotswold tour in a large motor carriage*'. Not to be outdone, the Mothers' Union of the nearby village of Dorridge '*were anxious to go to Stratford by road*'. This was door-to-door service which no other means of mass transport could provide. Gone forever were the days when a dog was known to sleep soundly and safely in the middle of Knowle High Street, for better or for worse, the rise of the motor vehicle had begun.

Chapter 3

'Cry "Havoc!" and Let Slip the Dogs of War'

From 'Julius Caesar' by William Shakespeare

The descent into war began with the murders of the heir to the throne of the Austro-Hungarian Empire, Archduke Franz Ferdinand and his wife Sophie at the hands of a Serbian member of the Black Hand Gang, a group of separatists who advocated murder as a method of achieving their aims. The Austro-Hungarian Empire delivered an ultimatum to the Serbian Government listing ten demands, eight of which were acceded to, leaving two to be negotiated. The British Foreign Secretary, Sir Edward Grey tried desperately to avert war, at a meeting with the German Ambassador to Great Britain, Prince Karl Max Lichnowsky, the two men realised that with very little effort, matters could be resolved to the satisfaction of all parties. But intransigence prevailed, massive armies were set in motion, millions were to die.

As mentioned previously, Great Britain did not have a formal agreement to go to the aid of France but was a signatory to the treaty which guaranteed the neutrality of Belgium. Once the German armies

Sir Edward Grey, Foreign Secretary.

had invaded Belgium, ignoring Britain's pleas to cancel their attacks and, with frantic calls from France to come to her assistance, the British Government felt that it had to commit the BEF to the escalating crisis. Britain had always feared the occupation of the continental North Sea and Atlantic coasts by a hostile power (a situation that came to pass in 1940). That night as the gas lamps in the Mall were being lit, Sir Edward remarked to a friend *'the lamps are going out all over Europe, we shall not see them lit again in our lifetime'*.

This would be a fitting place in the narrative to mention the contribution to MT for the BEF of one of the most famous names in the world of furniture, Waring & Gillow.

The firm occupied premises in Oxford Street, London. Twenty-four hours after the declaration of war, nine of the firm's 3-ton vans were recalled by telegram from as far afield as the Midlands and the South Coast, one van running non-stop from Worthing in Sussex. Immediately on arrival at Oxford Street, mechanics set to work to convert the vans' fuel systems from paraffin to petrol and change the sidelights from electric to oil lamps. The requisite stocks of spare parts required were already on hand and stowed on board, as were the tools needed to maintain the vehicles. Canvas fire-buckets, first aid kits, fire extinguishers and the regulation six spare cans of petrol, plus jacks were also supplied. The drivers were all members of the Army Reserve. A short speech to wish the drivers well was given by a *Waring and Gillow* official, then the convoy left at 11pm arriving at Avonmouth at 7am the following morning. This tremendous effort went on to be repeated in many parts of Great Britain; the nation was in peril and it was up to everyone to make some contribution, however small, to alleviate the situation.

The die was cast. Great Britain was about to become embroiled in a Western European war for the first time since 1815 which

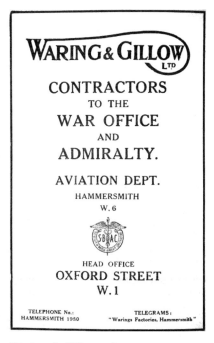

WARING & GILLOW LTD

CONTRACTORS
TO THE
WAR OFFICE
AND
ADMIRALTY.

AVIATION DEPT.
HAMMERSMITH
W. 6

HEAD OFFICE
OXFORD STREET
W. 1

TELEPHONE No.:
HAMMERSMITH 1950

TELEGRAMS :
"Warings Factories, Hammersmith"

Waring & Gillow advertisement.

A Waring & Gillow van deployed to Ypres 1914.

marked Wellington and Blucher's victory at Waterloo, achieved with a fearful 'butcher's bill'. Since the days of Waterloo, armies had grown to such a vast extent in personnel that they were now numbered in millions, except that is in Great Britain, which only retained a highly professional colonial police force said to have been called by the German Kaiser, '*a contemptible little army*'. The BEF which went to 'France' (it was always, somewhere in France) but fought its first battle in Belgium, was known to have the most accurate riflemen in the world, who were required to fire off fifteen aimed shots per minute using their famous Lee-Enfield .303 rifles. One reason for this amazing proficiency was that the British Government would not pay for the supply of more than a basic allocation of machine guns, which, firing at maximum speed, could deliver 600 rounds per minute per gun.

As was to become all too quickly apparent, the amount of ammunition consumed rose by prodigious amounts. In the case of the expert riflemen, their guns quickly became too hot to use; the only alternative being to pick up a weapon discarded by a wounded or dead comrade. For the ASC the uninterrupted supply of ammunition to the forward troops would become a huge problem due to the lack of suitable vehicles, whether horse-drawn or motor vehicles. The supply chain itself reached far beyond the base depots in France, it crossed the English Channel to the factories of the UK via the railway system then, on to the copper mines located in far-flung corners of the world, from whence it was transported in ships of the British Merchant Fleet, which itself became a major supply organisation without which victory would certainly not have been possible.

The BEF under Field Marshal Sir John French was safely conveyed to its ports of embarkation in a masterpiece of railway operations which allowed the railways to do what they do best – deliver large consignments over long distances.

Field Marshal Sir John French.

A total of 1,800 trains ran over four days to the ports of embarkation, troops to Southampton, food to Liverpool, stores to Newhaven and MT to Avonmouth. Colonel J.F.C. Fuller praised the railway and its highly professional servants, praise indeed from the usually acerbic Fuller who had been posted to Southampton docks to co-ordinate the embarkation. Commenting on an amusing incident when confronted by a very angry major protesting at limits imposed on his battalion's baggage allowance (the baggage in question was allowed to pass) led Fuller to remark that it was *'unpacked about one week later by Germans'*.

In total, upon the outbreak of war, only 200 MT vehicles were in regular, full time service with the army. All of the 700 motor vehicles in the 'subsidy' scheme were taken over immediately; unfortunately, but not surprisingly, many were found to be in a poor state of repair. Matters to overcome MT shortages were soon put in hand via a 'Confidential Register' which listed all MT that could be taken over by the government in a national emergency. New officers were commissioned who had been employed in the motor trade and knew their areas well. Lorries engaged on food distribution work were not taken up and manufacturers of goods vehicles were encouraged to increase production. In all cases, the War Office had first call on the new vehicles, at a pre-agreed price. Shipments of MT to France began as a matter of urgency, they were driven in many cases by drivers without any experience of the Army or, driving on the 'wrong side' of the road.

Field Marshal Sir William Robertson.

In August the truth that an army marches on its stomach became all too clear. In the month of August 1914, the tiny BEF required, 4,500,000 lbs of bread, 3,600,000 lbs of meat and 842,000 gallons of petrol. The horse fodder requirements outstripped all in weight and bulk and would do so for the entire period of the war. Fortunately for the BEF, it possessed in the person of Sir William Robertson, who rose from private to field marshal and became a quartermaster general of supreme professionalism, a man who quickly realised the challenges facing an army operating in a huge foreign landmass not of its own choosing. Supplies of food and ammunition had to be fast and reliable as troops without food quickly become a rabble ripe for defeat. Rifles without bullets and artillery pieces without shells are nothing more than scrap. For Sir John French to have the freedom to act or react to the enemy, his army must be well supplied. Now the time had come for the ASC and MT to show what it could do in the ultimate testing ground of all, that of war.

Shown below are some of the diverse range of vehicles that eventually served the BEF in France. It reads like a history of now, long-lost names from British industry; also shown are products of American, Italian and Swiss industry that played their part in keeping the BEF on the road.

Associated	British Quad	Hallford	Peerless
Equipment	Buick	Quadrant	Pierce-Arrow
Company	Cadillac	Karrier,	Riker
(AEC)	Clydesdale	Kelly-	Saurer
Alldays &	Commer	Springfield	Seabrook
Onions (still	Daimler	Lacre	Straker-Squire
existing)	Dennis	Leyland	Studebaker
Austin	Foden	Locomobile	Thornycroft
Belsize	Fiat	Maudslay	Vinot
British Berna	Garford	Pagefield	Wolseley

There were also four different makes of vans and five makes of ambulances, thirty-five makes of cars and nine makes of motor cycles. The number of vehicles expanded rapidly, but so did the need for a reliable supply of spare parts for the multiplicity of different makes. The vehicles that went to war were soon pushed far beyond the limits ever imagined by their designers in what was a relatively new technology. The image of a Maudslay lorry reveals an historic survivor; built in 1915, she saw service on the Western Front, served with the RAF and became a caravan in Scotland. She is now in the care of Coventry Transport Museum's expert staff who have restored this remarkable machine to running order. The lorry's engine contains several features widely used today including overhead camshafts, aluminium castings to reduce weight and a simple arrangement to adjust the timing of the engine.

Mechanical, electrical and body components wore out quickly, many breaking apart and leaving the vehicle stranded whereupon, in the eyes of the military, it had become a liability as opposed to an asset. Quick and efficient repair was required, the only other options being salvage for usable parts or, if the enemy was at hand, complete destruction to deny the enemy the advantage of a possible source of spare parts or, the payload the vehicle may have been carrying. The historian, Richard

Maudslay lorry, 1915.

Maudslay lorry engine.

British 'Berna' lorry.

Pullen described how in early 1915, Daimler received an order on a Monday for fifty, 2-ton lorries to be completed and ready for France by the following Saturday. By herculean efforts the lorries were finished, albeit with the last few leaving the factory before the paint was dry. In the case of Berna, a company based in Switzerland, agreements were made to buy up all the current and future vehicles manufactured in Switzerland so preventing any Berna products falling into hands of Germany, an arrangement that was in place until 1917.

Chapter 4

Into France and First Contact with Friends and Foe

Shoulder flashes displaying the letters RFA (Royal Field Artillery) were an early cause of friendly misunderstanding between the French civilian population and the BEF. The locals took RFA to mean the Triple Entente of Russia, France and Angleterre. The same well-meaning civilians cheered '*les Generals, Potash et Perlmutter*' a firm of London merchants whose advertisements were carried on the 'B' Type omnibuses carrying the BEF towards Mons. Crossroads were often 'guarded' by over enthusiastic men who looked old enough to have served in the Franco-Prussian War of 1870. One sentinel in particular, who was arresting all passers-by, eventually attempted to arrest a splendidly uniformed French staff officer; in seconds the would-be hero, who it was quickly discovered was more than a trifle inebriated, was reduced to tears and begging the staff officer for permission to go home and eat his supper. This is not to downplay the French reservists and territorials; only a few days later, they fought ferociously to the very end, suffering horrendous casualties on the left of the BEF. French history labels the fighting from first contact with the invader until the fight-back at the Marne in September as the Battles of the Frontiers. French casualties for the period numbered some 300,000, with 27,000 said to have been killed on 22 August alone. All the while the British were advancing towards the Belgian town of Mons through a gentle countryside of picture postcard villages surrounded by fields of golden corn and orchards heavy with the weight of abundant fruit.

In all one cavalry and six infantry divisions left British shores to concentrate in the area of Maubeuge, 13 miles south of Mons, the force numbering some 160,000 troops (of whom, 60 per cent were reservists) on the left flank of General Lanrezac's Fifth French Army. A forward move by the BEF began in order to reach the line of the Mons-Condé Canal just north of Mons which was attained on 22 August. In those days, the area was a very active coalfield intersected by numerous railway lines of standard and narrow gauge. Villages of closely packed terraced houses lined the largely unmapped roads which, without warning it seemed, would suddenly turn themselves into a cul-de-sac. Many a bold motor cycle despatch rider found himself inexplicably lost and unable to make himself understood. These same problems of navigation were to assail the ASC in the traumatic days to come. Very importantly for the BEF, troops were warned to keep off private property and not to make rifle loopholes in walls without permission from GHQ.

The military situation changed rapidly on 23 August when the BEF came into contact with the enemy and, by the troops' expert rifle fire, gave the Germans a bloody nose. Little did the British know their assailants were just the leading members of General von Kluck's First German Army. The BEF began to use up enormous stocks of ammunition with truly frightening rapidity; indents for re-supply began to pour into ASC forward detachments. Anything on wheels was sent forward with whatever supplies could be found only to discover that, in

'Commer Cars' advertisement.

the face of overwhelming odds, the army had begun to retire. Men and transport were streaming back, with walking wounded mixed up with helpless families fleeing in terror from the *Boche*, all clogging up the already inadequate road system. Lorries and vans loaded with badly needed food and ammunition became lost.

The hard lesson was soon learned that the vehicles could not go 'off road' to avoid the gridlocks. Drivers found themselves isolated without directions to the nearest supply dump that might still be operating. Often looked down upon by the fighting infantry, the ASC endured several uncomplimentary nicknames such as: Aunt Sally's Cavalry, Army Safety Corps and others. ASC drivers were paid initially at the rate of 6 shillings per day compared to the basic infantryman's remuneration of 1 shilling per day. It was widely but erroneously believed that ASC men were never in danger from the attentions of the enemy. During the Battle of Mons and the 200-mile retreat that followed, the ASC had numerous clashes with German cavalry. The drivers were not usually armed, their only defence being the speed of the lorry.

Another very real danger arose from 'jumpy' sentries. An incident recorded by A. Corbett-Smith in *The Retreat from Mons* told of an alarm being raised at 10pm of the approach of 'enemy troops' – that French farmer and his cow never knew how close they had come to oblivion. In another incident of mistaken identity in the area which would shortly become the German-held Leipzig Redoubt on the Somme battlefield, a farmer tending his herd of cows in the early morning mist, was shot dead by French troops who mistook him for a German. At least the troops apologised to his widow. Decades later, visitors to the Somme would often see the farmer's daughter, Rose, sitting in her garden, she would always wave and didn't mind at all if visitors wished to meet her.

Descriptions of narrow escapes by MT drivers were published in late 1914 by the ASC Journal described as 'various adventures' told by ex-bus drivers, van drivers and others. One 'adventure' began with a large column of loaded, heavy ammunition lorries which almost came to grief because of faulty map reading. This would have taken place before the continuous trench lines divided Europe from the North Sea to the Swiss frontier. The column had strayed into enemy-held territory and had been quickly spotted. Shells began to fall about the lorries and to add to their woes, German cavalry were quickly on the scene

Thornycroft London bus during the First World War – Mike O'Brien.

making determined efforts to surround and cut off the column. In a desperate measure, the officer in charge gathered all the lads into the first six lorries and set off in a race to beat the converging horsemen. The horsemen won and quickly set up a 'gauntlet' on both sides of the road expecting the column to surrender. The column officer was driving the lead lorry and in a forlorn hope kept the accelerator pedal hard down on the floor of the cab. The enemy now opened up with rifle and pistol fire at the oncoming lorries, bullets began to whistle by, but they pressed on. By a miracle the enemy broke and turned away, leaving the convoy to race for safety (probably at about 25 mph). Thankfully, none of the men received as much as a scratch.

Proving the veracity of the old saying 'Who Dares Wins' were the officer and three other ranks who were captured complete with their lorry about the same time as the 'adventure' mentioned above. The driver in this case was a London bus driver from Putney. The captives were told to bed down with their lorry by the roadside under the baleful eye of an infantryman appointed to act as their guard. Unfortunately for the German guard, but fortunately for the captives, said guard appeared to have been indulging in more than a few mind-altering beverages. As it grew dark, he was seen to slump to the ground and before long loud snores began to reverberate around the otherwise peaceful countryside. Seeing their chance, the captives very quietly prepared the lorry for starting and, in an all or nothing escape bid, started the engine and drove off westwards as hard as they could go, expecting at any moment volleys of rifle fire to follow them. But nothing happened to disturb the peace of the night and in an amazing escape they got clean away to the safety of the BEF lines.

Not all 'adventures' had agreeable endings. Again in late 1914 a lorry driver was blown to pieces when a shell entered his cab from the right-hand side. The driver's mate, who was also in the cab, escaped physical injury – what his mental condition was is not mentioned. The lorry itself was soon repaired and back in service, reflecting the already highly efficient MT recovery and repair organisation.

The rush to acquire motor vehicles for the BEF precluded any chance of repainting, so many were to be seen 'somewhere in France' sporting advertisements for Vaux Ales, corsets, margarine and many more. More vehicles were added to the fleet by purchasing second hand locally; owners were often only too pleased to sell to the BEF which paid good prices and did not complain if their newly purchased conveyance broke down. The document shown here is a good illustration of the practice of local purchase taking place even before the BEF had concentrated.

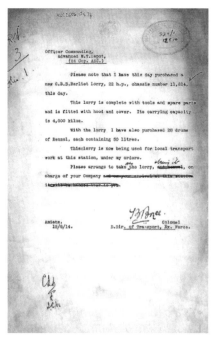

Lorry purchase document, Royal Logistics Corps Museum.

The retreat from Mons ended east of Paris. The Germans were but 23 miles from the French capital whose citizens could hear, with trepidation in their hearts, the sinister, distant booming of artillery. The French

Government was in crisis. In a desperate measure, lorries and 600 Paris taxi cabs were hastily requisitioned to rush troops to the battle front, an ultimately successful logistical operation that contributed to the denial of the capital to the invaders. On 5 September, the French Commander-in-Chief, General Joseph Joffre, launched a joint Anglo-French attack which became known as the Battle of the Marne (River Marne). The ASC Journal for August 1915 commented:

On the retreat from Mons, the ASC displayed its undefeatable character; shorn of the assistance on which it counted with roads blocked by retreating troops, never failed for a single day to wring the needful supplies from the railway and carry them to the fast melting army. On the retreat collapsed and fainting men, equipment, clothing and ammunition had been piled into empty lorries. When the Anglo-French armies struck back at the Marne and the previously all conquering enemy was put to flight, the BEF played a vital role. That it did so was due in no small sense to the lorries. Unkempt, uncleaned, caked with dust, and reeking of unpleasant odours, they just screwed down their greasers and carried on. There was no time to worry about big-end bearings, 'we either got there or bust up' one of the drivers said.

The speed of the advance was such that HT could not keep up, this included the horse-drawn ambulances. The only alternative was to use returning lorries to transport the wounded. The drivers found themselves to be urgently required in both directions, food, ammunition and reinforcements must go forward, rearward, the unfortunate wounded must be saved and handed into the care of the medical services. A round trip of a hundred miles became commonplace as was enduring three days without sleep. The screams of the wounded carried on the floor of the jolting lorries seriously unnerved many of the drivers; more so than near misses from shells. With the strain of ceaseless loading, driving, collecting and delivering the wounded, they were so utterly worn out that more than one collapsed, unconscious, while at work without a word of warning.

Another personal account comes from a letter written by a driver serving with 48 MT Coy. describing his experience of the Retreat from Mons:

I would not have thought it was possible to fall asleep while driving a lorry, that's what happened many times to us all on the retreat. We were so very tired out. At times when our column stopped for orders, we would fall fast asleep only to be woken by shouts that the enemy was not far off. The speed limit had to be ignored and broken-down lorries and vans had to be left behind.

The driver then went on to relate the problems caused by the weather:

Back in the early part of the war we had splendid dry weather, back then all the complaints were about dust which was awful, clouds of it with hundreds of motors travelling together. Now it has turned cold and we have had a lot of rain which has turned the roads to mud. We now slip and slide all over the roads.

Not that the invaders always had the initiative, as the following account reveals. One night about 11.30pm, a Frenchman accosted an MT sergeant to inform him that a party of Uhlans (much feared German cavalry) had billeted themselves in his farmhouse. The sergeant, being an adventurous sort, decided that the Uhlans should be captured. After waking up his men and calling for volunteers he set out, guided by the farmer, with his small party to carry out the raid. The enemy were taken completely by surprise and were only too willing to surrender. Their greatest fear was that they would be handed over to the French who had old scores to settle. Two of the prisoners were unable to walk as they had sustained wounds from the day before; a cart was quickly acquired to serve as a makeshift ambulance and the patients removed to safety.

The Battle of the Marne had seen the invaders repulsed but not ejected from France. However, the much-vaunted German Schlieffen Plan, which called for the encirclement and destruction of the French armies in 42 days, was in ruins, never to rise again. With the French right flank secure, a race began with each side trying to outflank the other; success would have allowed one side to loop around and destroy their enemy from three sides at once. Neither side could outrun the other, both sides reaching the Belgian coast at Nieuport by 20 October 1914. There the front lines would stay until 1918.

For MT a pattern of operations formed whereby MT would act as the vital link between the 'Heads of Steel', as railheads were known, and the 'refilling points' where HT would take over for the cross-country work of supply and so it would remain until the end of the war.

In the words of Corbett-Smith:

Regimental jealousy (if it ever existed) was obliterated completely, and every officer and man, from General Officers Commanding Corps to the 'bus drivers who drove A.S.C. lorries, worked shoulder to shoulder. And so, we pulled through.

The BEF had been in real peril of annihilation but, thanks only to the superhuman efforts of all ranks it lived to fight another day.

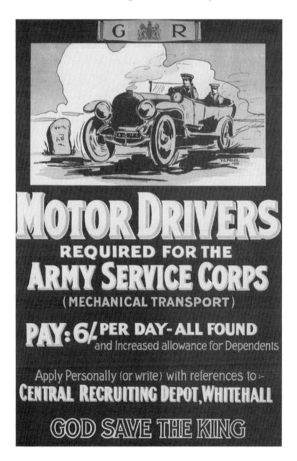

Recruitment poster.

October 1914 found 316 Coy despatching one motor lorry daily to collect stores from barges on the river and canal systems, another facet of BEF operations that is largely forgotten. The Inland Waterways Companies saved large amounts of petrol and freed up urgently required dock and warehouse space. November of 1914 saw the beginning of road deterioration as reports began to arrive of muddy, slippery and pot-holed surfaces. A fatal accident occurred in January 1915 when a civilian was killed by a lorry from 317 Coy, although in statements given by witnesses the driver could not have avoided the accident. Still with 317 Coy, on 3 March, Lance Corporal Williamson, while driving a Daimler 30 cwt lorry, collided with a handcart in Rue St Vulfran (possibly Arras) and broke a window of house No.13.

By March 1915, 316 Coy had been issued with sixty-two vehicles, the products of at least ten different manufacturers that included Thorneycroft. A note in the unit war diary states '*no provision for repair of vehicles but, 4 drivers and 2 fitters are to do repairs with the tools carried on the vehicles.*' The diary then tells us that there were no buildings in which to establish a workshop, so three empty trailers were found and lined up side by side. No machine tools were available but eventually a Douglas power and lighting set was obtained, machines issued but hand tools were not available from central stores. In February 1915 a Peerless lorry incorporating a mobile workshop appeared which must have been a great relief to all. Still in 1915, the unit set up a spare parts store to supply nearby units and passing vehicles in need of spares including tyres and accessories. The work of 316 was varied, transporting petrol to forestry works and five lorries on twice-weekly runs to take hospital linen to a French laundry were everyday tasks.

As the year turned 735 Coy began operating from 'a large covered workshop' where they made special vehicle bodies for forestry work. Timber was carried from the forests to sawmills to be cut into standard lengths. Very large logs were loaded by the use of block and tackle, everything was used with nothing going to waste. As the drivers would be away all day at considerable distances from camp, a packed lunch was supplied to be eaten while waiting to load and unload. A very welcome hot meal was provided upon return to camp.

Not all soldiers behaved in an exemplary manner. Private 07521 G.R. Hinton, was tried by court martial for drunkenness, the verdict not recorded. Tuesday 8 June records Private Lynes, '*fired a rifle at Circus Depot-sent under guard to hospital for observation*'. On 11 June the entry records '*Hughes and Linford sent to prison.*' Sunday 22 August records *'a constant trickle of men admitted to hospital; Circus Depot due to sanitary reasons'.* A September entry notes *'2 Ptes return from prison.'*

It seems that October was a busy month for sickness and discipline matters: 15 October found Private H. Loton drunk on guard duty, a heinous offence which would have rendered Loton liable to be shot had he committed the same offence in the front lines. Loton could count himself lucky that he was awarded twenty-eight days' Field Punishment No.1. The sentence involved being tied to a waggon wheel or post for one hour in the morning and the same in the evening. Similar punishments were used by the Argentine army against deserters and looters during their occupation of the Falkland Islands in 1982.

An interesting entry recorded that a 3-ton Pagefield lorry had been received from an Irish civil plate-laying gang and a 3-ton Daimler was issued in exchange. Security was not forgotten as a *'safe for the custody of Company monies and secret documents had been received from the Army Ordnance Department.'* Low level crime was a problem for the BEF but never to the extent that discipline broke down.

As an example of the ever-varying tasks of MT, a 'disinfector lorry' was despatched to a prisoner of war camp to help with a hygiene problem. Serious accidents could occur on even the most mundane duties; a man detailed to guard some materials waiting for transport was run over and seriously injured by a horse waggon that was being towed by a lorry. A moment's inattention could spell disaster in the danger zones; survival instincts took over when people heard the banshee wail of approaching shells and would look neither left nor right as they dived for the nearest available cover. Drivers also mentioned at that time how beautiful the scenery was in the undamaged areas, in stark contrast to the scenes of recent battles where dead soldiers and horses were scattered as if they had been caught in a mighty hurricane. The men had nothing but praise for the Sanitary Corps whose unsavoury duties included collection and burial of the dead.

In all this mayhem of exploding shells, damaged roads and the failings of a small minority of their fellows, the ASC stuck to its task. The soldiers of the BEF were allotted 3,500 calories per day of the best food available. This included, beef, bully beef, mutton, bacon (best quality Irish) butter, cheese, jam, tea, rum, salt, pepper and, of course, bread – all of the best quality and to be delivered with the precision of a good clock. Ill fed mass armies cannot be relied upon and morale withers away in perfect harmony with the dwindling presence of rations.

Chapter 5

Driving on the High Toby 'Over There'

(The 'Toby' High or Low, was a very old coach driver's term for the high or low road)

From the inception of animal-powered vehicles through steam locomotives to powered road vehicles, all have needed a person to act as driver. The rapid uptake of the motor vehicle soon revealed a serious shortage of experienced drivers. Compared to today's drivers, the lot of their predecessors was an onerous one. Before starting the engine, a long list of checks had to be made; as mentioned earlier, the driver had somehow to prevent water being introduced into the petrol supply when filling the fuel tank. Also, on the to-do list was the prevention of foreign bodies mixing with the petrol which would cause fuel lines to become blocked. Both of the above conditions were deemed to come about because the driver had been careless. For much of their time on the 'High Toby' the drivers had to negotiate unmade roads, without the benefit of power steering, power and anti-lock brakes and travelling on solid 'bald' tyres over *pavé* (cobbled) roads, often at night without lights of any kind as using the vehicle's rudimentary lamps could attract the attention of the enemy.

The driver's cab was not fully enclosed, there being no windscreen fitted or an 'official' heater although some drivers were known to modify the engine's

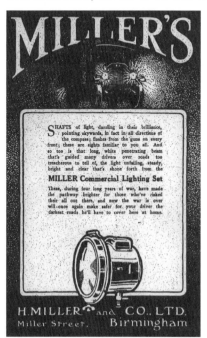

'Miller' motor lighting advertisement.

cooling system by diverting a hot water pipe from the engine to pass through the cab – all strictly against regulations of course but to be preferred to the alternative which was freezing. Gloves and the famous long, waterproof coat also helped to keep the driver reasonably warm. Goggles were another essential to keep the dust clouds of the dry season out of the eyes. The driver's seat would often as not be a single hard wooden bench leading many to provide their own means of padding to add a little comfort. Drivers working for Midland Red in the 1920s had to sit on the petrol tank and provide their own cushion.

Driving on solid tyres along deeply rutted roads caused severe jolting. In these road conditions, the steering wheel could be wrenched violently from the driver's grip and only through experience, or a willingness to listen by the novice to the advice proffered by older hands, could the risk of injury be curtailed. The undated poster shown here stresses the point that only experienced drivers need apply. It's also interesting to note that, *'No steam drivers need apply'* or, anyone with less than one year's driving experience – not easy conditions to fufill – as the services were already enlisting all the qualified drivers that they could lay their hands on. Note

that fitters and turners were also urgently required in order to keep the Army's vehicles on the road. A good turner was highly skilled at the use of a lathe, a rotating machine that could produce intricate cylindrical shapes to fine tolerances, and was a highly prized asset to the BEF when the lorry fleet had to be kept on the road at all costs.

In the words of Colonel Henniker on Great Britain's war transport arrangements: *'1914-18 bears the normal imprint of*

Motor Drivers (Car and Petrol Lorry) also good
Motor Fitters & Turners,
ARE REQUIRED FOR
Mechanical Transport, Army Service Corps.

ENLISTMENT.	For period of War only.
PAY.	6/- per day, all found, with separation allowance if married.
HOW TO JOIN.	Candidates for enlistment should present themselves at the Stoughton and Borough Hall Recruiting Offices between the hours of 10 a.m. and 6.30 p.m. on the 13th February, where they will be seen by a Mechanical Transport Officer. They should bring with them testimonials showing previous experience in motor driving. No applicants will be seen without references. Accepted men will be enlisted and required to proceed to the Mechanical Transport Depot on the following day.
IMPORTANT.	The Mechanical Transport Officer will be in for one day only, so candidates should not fail to present themselves on the 13th February between the hours mentioned.
	No Steam Drivers need apply, or Motor Drivers with less than one year's experience of driving.

God Save the King.

Recruitment poster for drivers.

British campaigns; begun on too small a scale, with very limited resources and with no provision for expansion.'

Many drivers and 'would be' drivers, better described as civilians in uniform, found themselves in a very active war zone with all its attendant dangers, driving vehicles that they were not at all familiar with. The driver becomes an integral part of the machine, pointing the vehicle in the required direction, stopping and starting as required being his main duties, being in effect the final link in the control system. Because drivers were human with all the unpredictability that goes with the species, rules governing driver behaviour on the road and the methods employed to obtain the best performance from both driver and vehicle were quickly formulated and constantly updated by experience.

Drivers' Orders (S.S. 400) produced by the Army Printing and Stationary Service runs to seven pages and was to be carried at all times by drivers of MT. The front page of the orders carries the warning, *'Always drive on the **Right** hand side of the road'*, followed by twenty-nine other headings describing the onerous responsibilities of the driver, who was also expected to carry out adjustments to the vehicle plus checking and replenishing of the oil, grease, water and petrol needs of his motor. Level crossings are referred to at length; the driver is cautioned not to attempt to cross the railway unless his exit is clear and never to open a crossing gate without due authorisation.

Graphically illustrating the wise words of Drivers' Orders, a driver from No.6 Auxiliary Petrol Coy (318 Coy ASC) came to grief on a level crossing when the Paris Express suddenly appeared out of the darkness. The first people on the scene found the lorry *'completely smashed; the locomotive overturned and two coaches derailed, by some miracle the lorry driver was found clinging*

ASC Driver Hudson, 1917. (Courtesy of R. Pullen)

to one of the locomotive's buffers, bruised but otherwise unhurt.' A close escape that should go down in history.

As well as Drivers' Orders the omnipotent hands of bureaucracy were never far away. The driver of any MT was under strict instructions to keep an official log book of the machine. Every facet of running and maintenance had to be recorded – fuel, tyres, spare parts, breakdowns, battle damage – all had to be faithfully logged until the day came when the vehicle was written off the books or destroyed by enemy action. Woe unto him who was found to be in possession of an incomplete logbook. S.S. 400 also added a piece of advice concerning a problem that we still have to this day: *'If approaching lights prevent a clear view (dazzled) of the road in front, drivers should halt their vehicles.'*

As to drivers sent directly to the front, the London bus driver was the most highly sought after. These men each had thousands of hours of invaluable driving experience on badly congested roads in all weather conditions. However, the men did not take readily to the finer points of army life; other ranks were forbidden to speak directly to an officer without there being an NCO present. The incident reported of a bus driver who enquired of his officer thus: 'I say boss, what about my

'Miller' & 'Lucas King of the Road' headlights.

MAY, 1918.   THE RADIATOR   11

THE VETERAN.

OFFICER (to recruit who has failed to salute): "Why didn't you salute me—how long have you been in the Army?"
RECRUIT: "All the morning, sir!!!"

Exchange of views, Officer & Private, see text.

dinner?' was handled with the greatest tactfulness by the young lieutenant. Or take the case of the sentry who failed to salute his CO; on the officer enquiring as to how long the soldier had been in the Army, the reply was 'all morning, sir'.

The case of the officer who approached two old bus drivers who were working under the bonnet of a 'B' Type, after dark 'somewhere in France' developed as follows. The officer enquired of the two men as to the purpose of their endeavours; there was no direct reply, only a question between the two men, 'who the ****** hell is that'? The reply being 'I don't know but I think he should **** 'orf.' To his credit, the officer conducted a discretionary retreat.

The bus drivers used the word 'turn' to describe a day's work, the present writer can vouch that 'turn' was still in use in the bus industry in the 1970s. The banter used in 1914 also survived into the 1970s; greeting a colleague in the pre-dawn starts would be accompanied by *'bin 'ere all night 'av yer?'* This was a reference to valuable overtime and often the added words of 'friendly' censure would be *'same old faces'*. Known as 'the good old six bobbers' the bus men were highly prized as skilful, reliable and trustworthy. However, such was the ever-expanding demand for more drivers that the supply of experienced men quickly expired. A means to overcome the shortage in France was the use of 'reinforcement drivers' who had recovered from illness or slight wounds who could drive a lorry loaded with supplies for a destination as required.

Unfortunately, many of these drivers failed to arrive at all or, became hopelessly lost or worse still, crashed. This entirely unsatisfactory situation led to the establishment by the War Department of driving schools. The first such school was opened in London in 1915 and run by the London General Omnibus Company using WD lorries. Problems arose as it became all too obvious that unsuitable men were being sent to the school – those of poor physique, some who were actually ill, and returning wounded. These men were complete novices at driving, convincing the pupils to watch the road ahead and not the pedals and levers on the floor of the cab proved to be a major headache for the instructors. On one occasion, an instructor told his pupil to sound the horn as he had spotted an elderly lady walking by the road; the pupil did sound the 'bulb' type horn by releasing his grip on the steering wheel and squeezing the bulb with both hands! The lorry veered off to the right narrowly missing a large motor car which was passing.

Night driving without lights, while wearing gas masks was also practised. All pupils had to pass through four grades before they were tested fit for service at the front. Some deemed unfit for the heavy work of a lorry were reclassified as 'Ford' that is, trained on Model T Ford vans which were required in large numbers by the services. Women were also trained for service with the Women's Legion, either as drivers or mechanic-drivers. Steam still had its place, men who could not master the lorry (usually because of the crash gearbox) or existing steam drivers, received instruction on all the types of engine in service with the Army. All the above mentioned courses included practical demonstrations and lectures on the inner workings of motors and steam engines. The courses usually lasted for six weeks, problems then occurred when the units the new drivers were despatched to, failed to fully trust the new people. Drivers were expected to negotiate narrow roads often with the surface 'crumped', that is riddled with waterlogged shell holes, in pitch darkness with shells bursting all around. Naturally, some men were terrified out of their wits when confronted by such circumstances for the first time but in the main and with tact and encouragement they pulled through to become trusted members of their company.

It was also noted in early 1915, before the establishment of driving schools, men were being sent out to France who had never driven a lorry, they could though drive a Ford van and, given the pressing need for drivers, they would have to manage. Many made good, others were despatched to other duties. Driver training is beautifully summed up in *The Radiator* a magazine published by the ASC during the Great War:

> *It's easy for a driver when his gears are shifting right,*
> *But the man's got grit who can calmly sit when his clutch is jammed up tight;*
> *For the test of an MT learner is an engine that's hoary with years,*
> *And the difficult part of the driver's art is to shift without grinding the gears.*
> *Your 'busman-instructor from Blighty is apt to say things that are hard*
> *When you double declutch on your hill test and the bus runs back a yard.*
> *Oh, the Strand's the place for the learner, or down through Oxford Street,*
> *For it makes him long to be home again.... or travelling on his feet.*

Attributed to Private R. Thomson – we hope he came safely home.

Many of the former London bus and taxi drivers who were early volunteers for the ASC, were noted for their extensive and 'crisp' vocabularies as would have been used when caught up in one of London's monumental traffic jams. It was also suspected that a number of drivers had lied about their age – not that they were too young to be on the Western Front, but too old. When an elderly looking driver was asked his age, he replied 42. As the driver was wearing the ribbon of the Egypt campaign of 1882, it was quietly pointed out that he would have been eight years old when he was awarded the medal; not to be deterred, the 'Old Sweat' carried on.

An interesting account of daily life in an MT depot during a quiet period tells of people sleeping in the backs of lorries being woken at 5.45am by the guards banging the sides of the lorries with rifle butts. A quick wash was followed by a short parade before the 'cookhouse is attacked,' fried bacon and hot tea being the staple fare. Three very good meals per day were available; many of the other ranks fed far better than they ever had in civilian life. Consider the fact that the average recruit weight gain in the BEF was 19lbs and in many cases a 3-inch increase in stature. Some men were accommodated in tents with those who were apt to grumble. The same account recommends that *'all grumblers be put in the trenches to open their eyes, this is a war, not a holiday'*. In some cases, formality was a little relaxed as officers and men made life a little more bearable by mutually dropping the conventions of class and all pulling together. The showing of 'side' was frowned upon, it being believed that those who displayed 'side' only showed themselves up. That said 'orders were orders' and both men and officers knew where the line had to be drawn, otherwise the old adage 'familiarity breeds contempt' would rear its ugly head.

Private T. Meek (allegedly so) published an account in *The Radiator* magazine of his experiences when learning to drive a lorry:

In civil life I was Secretary of the 'Addlepated' and District Window Cleaners Benevolent Society and a collector of moths. Motors, alas, were a thing outside of my world. On my first day's instruction when my hands touched the wheel, I knew I was up against it. I could see clutches everywhere, but my left foot consistently failed to find one. I was never sure which way the front wheels turned. The speed lever and the handbrake changed places in a startling fashion (or so it seemed). The engine stopped as and when it pleased and my efforts to 'swing her' became a shear [sic] torture.

My first 'blind' reverse made my heart stand still, every inch I went back was an inch nearer to destruction. My attempt ended when I hit a solid brick wall. My first encounter with traffic came about as I passed through Brentford on a busy day. In his efforts to prevent collisions, my instructor yelled 'Clutch out' and stamped on my left foot (clutch out means press the pedal down) *without an apology. I have a hazy recollection that my right hand was multiplied by four, as without warning, I blew the horn, manipulated the speed lever, and released the brake simultaneously.*

I was becoming too confident and with misplaced nonchalance, and ignoring advice to the contrary, I attempted to pass between two vehicles and bumped one. Turning to my instructor, I exclaimed that, 'there was oceans of room', 'yes', he replied, 'for a gnat.' I held my peace for he knew the 'Book of Words' better than I.

Following a night spent without sleep, the day dawned for my test. The time quickly passed; if the gears had been fur-lined, they could not have engaged more quietly. And so, in a blaze of glory I passed out.

Tonight, in the humid twilight, I shall waylay a few moths.

That Accusing Blue Eye: A Wealth of Expression Contained in One Look from the Instructor
(The Radiator 10 December 1916)

'Come on, Mate,' he rapped out to me as soon as his party had been checked by the wax-moustached gentleman with the book. 'Start her up' – just that, delivered staccato-like but oh! the agony and the straining and grunting it brought. The first inexperienced heave on the starting handle, the breathless defeat when the engine failed to start, the aching muscles and blistered hands.

Somehow the lorry engine was persuaded to start followed by a brief flicker from his deep blue eye to enquire why the engine was racing flat out and the lorry had not moved an inch? Eventually, and with a jerk, the lorry plunged forward like an express train then, suddenly making an abrupt halt which pitched the other trainees in the back of the lorry hard up against the cab. 'Take your foot off that throttle,' buzzed through my head and ever that accusing blue eye was upon me. He knew so well what ought to be done, and how, and I have discovered since that it was merely his keen desire that I too should know, that made him impatient with my blunders. Now I have got to know him a little better and my skills have developed somewhat, I've noticed that the look from the blue eye is occasionally accompanied by the hint of a smile.

In answer to a question (allegedly) submitted by a reader of *The Radiator: 'Searcher', No you are quite wrong about the instruction of M.T. drivers, being that they are born bad and grow worse.*

Finally, on the very important subject of driver training, *The Radiator* of March 1917 offered the following advice to learner drivers:

The whole art of driving lies in starting, diverging and stopping properly. A cool head, a keen eye, a sense of the speed at which one is travelling, and a knowledge of one's powers of stopping are the main factors necessary to the making of a successful driver.

DON'T expect other road users to perform the expected and correct thing. The unexpected always happens.

DON'T forget there are other people in the road beside yourself. Do not force a nervous cyclist on to the slope of a greasy road; drive cautiously when passing horses; do not race electric trams – an electric tram can get away faster and stop far quicker than you can.

DON'T forget when you meet bright lights to look straight ahead over the bonnet of your lorry.

High quality advertisement for Lucas 'King of the Road' lamps.

DON'T forget, when overtaking anything, to let your divergence from the straight be gradual. Do not go right up to the vehicle then pull out sharply. Do everything gradually. Start gradually, stop gradually, diverge from your straight line gradually.

Some sound advice for the new driver:

Do not boast of narrow escapes in your letters home, this is bad luck as fiction can become reality, think of Jules Verne and submarines. Do not use bad language in front of your lorry; she is a lady after all. Should you wish to impress, wear a very large revolver (ammunition optional). Try to speak French, beer is rendered bee-air, you will soon learn more. Do not complain if by some outside chance you are given a run to a hot-spot, this is only temporary, our mates in the infantry have to stick it out and they don't complain.

In 1915 there was a call for MT drivers to volunteer for transfer to 771 Company ASC. The men who volunteered discovered that they were to re-train as 'tank' drivers, whatever that meant. Came the great day, 15 September 1916, when tanks were first put to use in action, all of the drivers were ASC men and wore their cap badge to prove it.

From *The Radiator*, March 1917, 'Hydraulics' – '*Yes, a camel can live for three weeks without a drink. But who wants to be a camel?*'

Driving Under Fire

From the earliest days of the war it quickly became starkly evident that nowhere was safe in the accepted form of the word, as long-range guns could easily hurl high explosive shells at distances up to 18 miles. Stray shrapnel bullets were known to strike a single soldier amongst a group, none of whom even heard the shell coming or the subsequent explosion. Poison gas drifted for several miles killing or disabling everything in its path; all living things, including plants, became victims of the evil clouds. ASC men were not in a position to retaliate or even to instantly dive for cover. MT had to be brought to a halt and secured by the hand-brake before those on board made a rapid exit, to do otherwise risked being run over by their own or someone else's vehicle.

Just outside Ypres in December 1914, a column of lorries was brought to a halt by the sight of enormous eruptions taking place on the road ahead. A cloud of black smoke reached about 600ft into the air accompanied by road material and shell splinters. Nearby was a 6-inch gun manned by the Royal Garrison Artillery; a gunner advised the ASC men to get under cover as the enemy was firing 'Coal-Boxes' hence the black smoke clouds. Seconds later, three of the infernal devices burst with massive, thunderous double-roars and the showering of red-hot shell splinters for a little time after. As so often happened, the new men began foraging for souvenir shell splinters quickly discovered that the objects of the hunt were too hot to handle. When the column eventually resumed the journey, severe headaches were widely reported by the men but strangely when they came under fire again, the headaches had all but disappeared.

Ypres features often in early accounts of MT as it was the main operating area of the BEF in late 1914. The ASC witnessed the slow destruction of the city as the British refused to concede it to the enemy. Noted on one occasion, a shrapnel shell burst nearby on the road, quickly followed by a little boy who ran out of his house to look for souvenirs, very fortunately the shell was not followed by another. As the lorries passed through Ypres, along streets of houses ruined by the endless shelling, the heads of the occupants would pop up from the cellar gratings to watch the convoys pass.

The lorry was already, in late 1914, demonstrating its ability to negotiate the ever more 'crumped' roads. The crumps (shell holes) quickly filled with water added to which, the soil from the holes was spread over a wide area and turned into the ubiquitous mud. A junior officer told of the skills of the lorry drivers in avoiding crumps that were 4-5ft deep, and at the same time not

Private Arthur Pullen, A.S.C. 1915.

getting bogged down while shells exploded as close as 50 yards away. The souvenir hunters quickly got to work finding shell splinters up to 8 inches long and 1 inch thick. According to the officer, the noise of these particular shells arriving sounded like a piece of 'rending calico' (cotton cloth being ripped).

Three ASC men had an eventful trip when attempting to deliver rations. Darkness had fallen when the trio and their van came upon a large column of French artillery on the road. The driver knew the area and was able to make a detour, regaining the route only to discover that the intended recipients of the rations had by now moved 3 miles further away. There were numerous French soldiers about who informed the crew that the enemy was very near and all lights must be extinguished immediately. They decided to push on with one man walking beside the van, but the darkness was so complete that it was judged too dangerous to drive further. Leaving one of their number to guard the van, the driver and his mate elected to walk forward and try to find the whereabouts of the troops needing the rations. They eventually reached a village that was under intense rifle fire. Taking shelter behind a wall, they could hear English being spoken but could see no faces. Luckily, they heard a voice that they recognised, that of a sergeant major; between them and by speaking to 'shadows' they finally found they were able to explain the situation directly to the sergeant major who quickly realised the urgency of the situation and organised men and hand carts to collect the much-needed food. The men arrived back at base with the van just in time to prevent a search party setting out to look for them. Only months before, the three men had been employees of Sunlight Soap, London General Omnibus and British Cab Car – a transformation of a day's work indeed.

Another anonymous account published by *The Times* on 27 February 1915 tells us:

A few evenings back came an urgent order from the Engineers for a large number of sandbags, and I took charge of the convoy which was to do the work. We had first to go to a railhead about 19 miles off. That part of the work was easy enough, as the roads were good, and I knew them well; all went well until we got about four miles from our destination. Then the roads began to get very narrow, with constant turns, in addition to which they were very greasy. It was absolutely necessary for the lorries to keep right in the centre of the road. The least deviation meant their slipping sideways, as the road was very highly cambered, and several times they did slide sideways, although going very slowly, into thick mud at the roadsides. This meant towing out the one stuck, which was not usually a difficult job, but on one occasion the two leading lorries got stuck at once. The second one, being heavily loaded with sandbags and up to its axles, could not be pulled out by the lorry behind until its load of 6,000 sandbags had been taken off. It was then pulled out backwards and when free it proceeded to pull out the leading lorry, also backwards, of course, after which it was loaded up again.

While this was going on several batteries situated at short distances from both sides of the road we were on opened fire on the German lines, and for half-an-hour were very busy. We could see a good many of the shells bursting over the enemy's lines, but the village directly in front of us for which we were making, obscured our view considerably, as most of the shells went over it. The Germans began using their big searchlight while we were freeing the lorries to locate our batteries, which were however, too well hidden to be seen: the beams passed just over our convoy, so they did not discover it, which was fortunate. Owing to its [the convoy's] *inability to move it would have been a good mark for the German gunners and probably all that could have been saved would have been my car which was about 100 yards ahead of the leading lorry. Eventually we reached our destination in the village in which nearly every house was more or less damaged, and which is shelled most days, delivered our load, and returned to our quarters without further incident.*

The ASC never, if it was in their power, let the infantry down.

In a post war interview quoted here verbatim, an MT driver remembered:

Evidently they were short of drivers. Probably they'd had a lot of casualties, I don't know. But four or five of us went from the battery to help, to join the DAC (Divisional Ammunition

British soldiers collect food for horses. (Courtesy of R. Pullen)

Column). Our job there was supplying the guns. You had to find what ammo' you wanted and take it yourself. We got it from the dumps in the neighbourhood where they were. We had some tricky little jobs. Sometimes the guns were up the side of the infantry. Well, in that case it meant going up very quietly in the middle of the night, you know. You can guess how it was with the ground all chewed up with mud and, oh the mud. Mud-mud was the enemy.

Wars can have their lighter moments as the 'B' Type bus proved. Built for the city, these buses developed a singularly embarrassing habit. When engaged on out of town work, they collected mud in prodigious quantities. As soon as town boundaries were crossed, and the roads became surfaced with pavé, the 'B' Type obligingly and very quickly divested itself of its cargo of mud. On one occasion a very smartly dressed corporal was, much to his loud and intemperate displeasure, quickly turned into an unrecognisable disgrace. Not to be outdone, another 'B' Type moved slightly up-market and gave the same treatment to a sergeant-major who, by the use of unprintable nouns and adjectives proceeded to pour scorn on the driver's lineage. An anonymous commentator remarked that the 'B' Type in question was a true democrat as it could just as easily have ruined a field marshal's day. Small wonder then that the excellent 'B' Type soon acquired the alternative title of 'Mud Slinger'.

ASC Drivers were assigned to a multiplicity of tasks including that of driving ambulances under fire. On its return from the front, one ambulance was reported to have 180 holes in the bodywork caused by bullets and shell splinters. The fates must have been smiling that day as no-one was hurt by the flying metal and the ambulance was quickly repaired and put back into service.

Private R.G. Masters, an ASC driver, was awarded the Victoria Cross for his work, he volunteered to take an ambulance forward when communications had been lost and many wounded were stranded without hope of rescue. Private Masters made multiple journeys, threading his way through debris and constantly under shell and machine-gun fire plus a bomb dropped by an enemy plane, to reach the helpless wounded. A native of Southport, Private Masters was one of five brothers serving in the armed forces. A considerable amount of money amounting to £500 (£14,528) was collected on behalf of Private Masters, his wife and three children. The monies were invested, and interest paid monthly direct to the family.

Private R.S. Davies was awarded the Distinguished Conduct Medal in recognition of his gallantry when driving a loaded ambulance through a barrage of gas shells and machine-gun fire. The petrol tank was twice holed but luckily failed to ignite. In order to keep moving, Private Davies instructed one of the wounded to keep filling the tank from a spare can of petrol as a prolonged stop would not have been wise course of action, as they were under observation by the enemy. A short time later, the ambulance became 'bogged' and with no other alternative means to rescue his charges, Private Davies and one other soldier, physically carried all the wounded to safety despite shells bursting around them. Courage under fire was a job requirement for the ASC who were often accused (falsely) of avoiding such inconveniences.

MT and the lady drivers who risked all

Although not serving in the ASC, the following people/organisations made full use of MT to bring help to the wounded and remove them from the battlefield as quickly as circumstances permitted.

American humanitarian charities played an important role on the Western Front almost from the beginning of the war. Fully equipped and staffed purpose-built motor ambulances were shipped across the Atlantic to France where they were gratefully received; the courage and devotion of the volunteer doctors and nurses was often remarked upon.

Elsie Knocker and Mairi Chisholm were drivers of motor ambulances on the Western Front who went on to set up and operate the only front-line medical facility manned by women during the entire war. Both women survived despite the unwelcome attentions of enemy snipers and artillery.

Lady Dorothie Feilding also took enormous risks driving her ambulance. Much decorated, in 1915 she was the first woman to be awarded the Military Medal and would go on to receive the 1914/15 Star, Victory Medal, *Croix de Guerre* and the Order of Leopold. Besides shell and small arms fire, the ladies had to cut their hair short in an effort to combat the endemic plague of head lice. Dorothie survived the war, she died on 24 October 1935 at Mooresfoot House, Tipperary, Ireland, aged 46, and is buried in the Roman Catholic cemetery, Monks

Elsie, Mairi and Wolseley ambulance.

Kirby, Warwickshire. The photo depicts Lady Dorothie on the occasion of receiving her medal, February 1915.

During the same period, London County Council placed advertisements for Motor Ambulance Drivers. Preference was to be given to MT ASC drivers unfit for further active service – proof, if needed, of the good name of ASC drivers.

'Girl' drivers

In 1917, a 'Girl' driver reported her experiences of working for a commercial haulage company. She used the term 'Girl' throughout her report.

Lady Dorothie Feilding.

She had spent a full year working in the garage to get a good hands-on grounding in how MT worked. Out of respect for her feelings, the proprietor introduced a no swearing rule which if broken incurred a fine of 2/6d (12½p). The youngest lad in the garage was paid 5s per week (25p) leading him to complain that he could 'only afford two swears a week'. The Girl went on to drive the firm's 3-ton lorries in all weather and light conditions, describing the vehicle's lights as of little use on dark country roads. Apparently, the lights were known as 'Police Protectors', in what context she does not say. She comments on *'Youths of 17'* who although possessing the ability to drive well, insist on thrashing the vehicle with the seemingly held ambition to *'ruin the car in a month'*.

The Girl recommended good road manners at all times: *'Never pass a broken-down vehicle without offering to help, either a tow or, offer to phone the driver's employer from the next available telephone,'* the thanks of the stranded driver *'being worth more than money'*. These Girls made a major contribution to the war effort.

WRAF drivers.

Under Water (almost)

The lorry driver on the Western Front could easily find himself engaged in tasks far removed from carrying supplies. An incident occurred when the driver of an unladen 5-ton lorry, reacting to a car crash in front, wrenched the wheel over to avoid the survivors and in doing so climbed the bank of a canal, ran over the top of the bank and came to a halt with the bonnet and driving seat under water. In a state of shock, the lucky driver was able to escape through the back of his cab which consisted of just a canvas curtain. It was said that had the cab been fitted with a solid wooden back, the driver would most likely have been drowned.

There being no dedicated recovery vehicle available, the only alternative was to despatch three lorries equipped with ropes and planks of wood. By herculean efforts, a plank road was constructed behind the stranded lorry and the three rescue vehicles were attached. With a mighty heave the lorry was pulled through the soft top of the canal bank and down on to the busy road where, rescued and rescuers were not at all popular with the cars and lorries caught in the grid-lock. After a few hours the stranded lorry and its driver were pronounced well and continued on their way.

Slipping or skidding into ditches was an ever-present danger as the roads were often narrow and badly cut up with drainage ditches at either side. Trying to avoid oncoming traffic on a two-way road, most of which had very soft verges, could lead to the surface collapsing under the weight of the lorry which would then slide sideways into the ditch. One such case mentions twenty men spending eight hours to retrieve a lorry stranded in a roadside ditch. In Flanders, water was never far away, the water table being only 18 inches below the ground surface. Trenches which protected soldiers from rifle and machine-gun fire often cut through the natural flows of underground water causing yet more problems with surface drainage. Also adding to the water problem, the heavy shells would break through the clay layer below the surface releasing water under pressure to add to the flooding.

Arguably the greatest publication of the war, *The Wipers Times,* reported that two German submarines had been destroyed on the notorious Menin Road with another captured complete with crew. The same edition tells of a fleet of trawlers operating in Zillebeke as the village had been cleared of U-boats. If all of this dark humour seems excessive, the meaning of Flanders is 'The Flooded Land.' *The Wipers Times* first appeared in 1916 and ran for twenty-three editions, changing its title as the 'editorial team' were moved to different locations in the course of their military duties. The *Times* was famous for its spoof adverts, tongue-in-cheek advice and snippets of 'news' that might just have a ring of truth, as this from the July 1916 *Kemmel Times*:

> *Things we want to know; The name of the subaltern who told the Major that to take his wife to Nottingham Goose Fair was like taking a sandwich to the Lord Mayor's Banquet.*
>
> *'Tommy: Yes. If you hang your sock on the parapet on Xmas Eve you are likely to get something in it – or you – when you go to fetch it.*

Tricks of 'Cold Starting'

In the twenty-first century there are many drivers who have never used a manual choke to cold start a vehicle. The choke cut off most of the air supply to the engine, by doing so, the air and fuel mixture became what was known as 'rich' and hopefully, much more likely to explode inside the cylinders, thereby starting the engine. Most vehicles of First World War vintage did not have the benefit of a choke so drivers had to rely on other means to coax their engines into life on freezing mornings.

What follows was actually witnessed by the present writer up to the early 1970s, a period when, in order to own a car, people would buy anything on wheels, even wrecks that should have gone to the scrap yard years before.

The 'trick' in question involved pouring some petrol into a tin then setting light to it. After a few seconds the lid was placed on the tin which smothered the flames. The now warm petrol was poured into the engine's carburettor which mixed fuel and air, a good vigorous swing on the starting handle and, hey presto, the engine bursts into life – or with luck it might. A tin containing petrol-soaked rag, set alight and held against frozen engine water jackets was also applied as a desperate measure. Some units used the 'trick' of concentrating on the starting of one lorry then using it to tow start the next, which would then tow start its neighbour and so on. With or without chokes, cold engines could

Experiencing starting problems.

'flood', that is when more petrol has entered the cylinders than can be burnt at the correct time which causes the engine to stop. Another old 'trick' that our Great War drivers would have been familiar with when dealing with a flood, was to remove the spark plugs and hold a piece of lighted rag on a stick over the holes, stand clear and watch the jet of flame leap out as the petrol found some air to mix with – rough, ready and dangerous, but it worked right up to the 1970s. Finally, the last-ditch effort witnessed by the writer involved removing the sparking plugs and heating them in a domestic oven. Gloved hands refitted the plugs in record time and attempts to start the engine resumed; usually, in the writer's experience, followed by failure.

MT had to overcome unskilled staff, inexperienced drivers and vehicles of rudimentary quality, but dedication and sheer hard work brought its rewards and the BEF's transport system quickly evolved. While the railways became the strategic bulk carriers, MT fulfilled the role of tactical carrier and HT became the off-road link.

Cold starting a Peerless (Fearless Peerless) is described by Richard Pullen from an original Peerless handbook. The instructions commence thus:

> *Fill the radiator, the gasoline (petrol) tank and the oil reservoir. Set the gasoline tap to 'Supply'. Fill all the grease cups and oil at the points indicated on the lubrication chart. Check the crank case oil level. Set the hand brake. Be sure that the speed control lever is set at the neutral position. Set the throttle lever to a point 1½ inches up the quadrant. Set the spark lever in its lowest position. Unlock the spark switch at the dash coil with the key and turn to position 'B'. With the starting handle at its lowest position, push in and with a short quick upward motion turn the crankshaft one half revolution in a clockwise direction. Repeat this operation four times, thus filling all of the cylinders with explosive mixture. If anything is at fault with your setting of the ignition system, the charge in the cylinders is liable to fire too early, thus causing an engine Kick-back.... **this may result in a broken wrist**. Once the engine is started, take to your seat and speed up the motor for a moment to make sure that the oil is well splashed around the crank case.*

In addition, Peerless advised:

> *Don't run the lorry without oil, water and gasoline.*
> *Don't run the lorry in tram tracks, this will grind the edge off the tyres.*
> *Don't try to run over small objects in the road, this is expensive fun.*
> *Don't allow the lorry to stand on a hill without putting a wheel scotch in place, there are some people around who would release the hand brake.*

At this point we shall leave the story of the lorry pioneers to explore other issues that directly affected MT before we return again to driving as the story unfolds.

Chapter 6

Roads: Who Built Them – Repaired Them – Policed Them?

A lorry needs a driver to act as its 'brain', it also needs a firm smooth surface to run on in order for it to fulfil its potential. These points may seem obvious but, as we have already discussed, the supply of competent drivers became problematic in the early part of the war and so did the roads on which the lorries were expected to run. The tactical problem was a fairly simple one: how to cater for millions of men who were living in the open and needing all the necessities of life and war, delivered to their doorsteps without fail. Complications soon arose as the men were scattered in lines across hundreds of miles of open country accessed by very few, narrow lanes which often had no surface dressing at all and became impassable after rain or snow. Now add the presence of an equal number of hostile soldiers occupying lines opposite to those of the BEF and who were bent upon its destruction, and we have before us the one, most important problem for the ASC – how to deliver the goods without the men being killed or the horses and motor vehicles being destroyed.

The immediate answer had to be more and better roads and the means to build, improve and repair them, all of which, as we will see, used up men, machines and materials in prodigious quantities.

Transport problems had been brewing for the BEF for many months, in late September 1915, the ill-fated Battle of Loos conducted by First Army, had been beset with problems caused by severe road congestion leading to shortages of supplies of all descriptions. The grid-locked roads also prevented the vital move forward of two divisions of reserve troops (21st and 24th) who could only move forward at the pace of the traffic jams. Two 'UP' roads were allotted to the divisions, but these were also being used by HT and MT. The 21st Division, found itself on the road with traffic against it or coming from behind and not under

The never-ending road repairs, Northern France.

control. Seven crossroads and joining streams of traffic had to be negotiated, plus five level crossings which caused constant hold-ups.

The 24th Division had a very similar experience in that it had been allotted a 'DOWN' road to go 'UP', and both had to break formation as the roads were of insufficient width to accommodate large vehicles and the marching columns in their standard four abreast marching order. A division in standard marching order took up 15 miles of road, with breaks down to two abreast to pass traffic. In darkness and pouring rain, the strain on the men must have been almost unimaginable. When the reserves did eventually reach their operating areas, they were cold, wet, tired and hungry and in no condition to storm forward against a powerful and well-entrenched enemy. In fact, they did just that but with disastrous results. It should be pointed out that the staff of First Army and XI Corps were not Staff College trained, they just had to do their best in the most terrifying circumstances. The Staff College course was a two-year full-time commitment open only to experienced regimental officers. With the rapid expansion of the Army the staff courses had to be placed in abeyance.

As the year 1915 ended, the BEF could look back on a year of disappointments: the immortal city of Ypres had only just been held with great losses; many of the Old Contemptibles had gone to their graves, bringing home that old truth *'The paths of glory lead but to the grave.*' The battles of Neuve Chapelle, Aubers Ridge and Loos had all failed in their objective, which had been to act in conjunction with the French Army to expel the invaders from France and Belgium. Hill 60 near Ypres had been won and lost. The 'Hill' was a man-made feature originally 750ft in length and 197ft above sea level and one of two such hills composed of spoil from the nearby railway cutting. Known locally as *Côte des Amants* (Lover's Knoll) it was, unusually for Ypres, not waterlogged and gave good observation over the enemy. Such was the importance given to Hill 60, that as a child the writer's mother could remember the commotion when news of actions at the hill reached her Durham coal mining village.

For the ASC the work of supply was always the same, expanding as the armies grew in numbers of men and still further when a 'show' was looming and the tempo increased accordingly. In April 1915, the ASC Journal reported:

Our Brigade has suffered heavily in the severe fighting, and some of the very best fellows, with whom we were dining on the previous night, have fallen on Hill 60. Never in my life do I wish to hear such terrible shaking of the earth as we are experiencing now, and still less do I want to see such awful, unmentionable sights as I saw at Ypres three days ago. Thank God, I got my supply section out without a casualty. I recommended two of our fellows for conspicuous coolness and courage. Our waggons were used for the conveyance of dead and wounded to the hospitals.

In his despatch of June 1915, Field Marshal French remarked:

In this despatch I wish to again remark upon the exceptionally good work done throughout this campaign by the Army Service Corps...not only in the field, but also on the Line of Communication and at the base ports.

To foresee and meet the requirements in the matter of ammunition, stores, equipment, supplies and transport has entailed on the part of the officers, non-commissioned officers and men of these Services a sustained effort which has never been relaxed since the beginning of the war, and which has been rewarded by the most conspicuous success.

By the late summer of 1915, the BEF had taken over some of the French positions in the Department of the Somme, not actually on the river of that name. The BEF's lines of communication were considerably extended and, very importantly, the means of reaching the troops in the new forward areas had to depend largely on the road and country lane system that the visitor finds to this day.

In all that follows, it is worth recalling the words of two people who took part in the Battle of the Somme, firstly, Colonel M.G. Taylor, Assistant Director of Movements who, in a lecture given shortly after the war remarked:

When it is possible to study the Great War as a whole, and as a matter of history, it will be found that many of our earlier troubles were due to the imperfect grasp of this truth. Transportation was the cause of our greater difficulties – not fighting power, leadership, or the more active side of military training.

Secondly, Charles Carrington, a Royal Warwickshire officer who in his *Soldier from the Wars Returning* echoed Colonel Taylor's thoughts:

His (Haig's) limiting factor was the physical problem of conveying men, guns, ammunition, and stores to the place where they could be used. Even more than he needed aeroplanes and tanks, he needed locomotives, sidings, plank roads, hutments, and timber.

We used to call the captain's horse a charger, but by 1916 it's more probably a pony impressed from a milk float.

Where roads on the Somme existed at all they, in common with many British roads, were water sealed, the fine dust mixed with water and rolled to produce a surface crust that dissolved with rain or billowed up into clouds of dust in dry weather. Chalk abounds on the Somme, an ideal material for producing dust with the added distinction of turning to a glue-like substance when mixed with water. The accumulation of dust in the inner workings of motor vehicles could lead to electrical breakdowns besides bringing great discomfort to the driver in his open cab. The dust was also causing another and far more serious and possibly life-threatening problem. The prominent clouds of dust were of great interest to hostile eyes observing from the other side of no man's land. Even the regulation speed of 10 mph was more than enough to produce tell-tale clouds which became prime targets for artillery observers. As the enemy were in possession of the same area maps as the BEF, they knew the ranges of the roads to a yard, making movement along them very dangerous indeed. When shells began to precede or follow the vehicle, the driver could only hope that the German gunners were not very quick on altering the range or firing angle. Great were the discussions among ASC personnel as to the merits of travelling slowly so raising less dust but offering a slow-moving target or, travelling faster, raising more dust but be harder to hit. Many drivers opted for higher speed as experience showed that the incoming shells most often fell behind the vehicle. New drivers who opted to travel slowly to reduce the dust menace quickly 'stood on the gas' when the very unwelcome attentions of the enemy began to arrive, and who could blame them?

Roads that were 'open', that is, known to be under observation by the enemy, were particularly dangerous as they were susceptible to machine-gun fire. An experienced machine gunner could follow his stream of bullets and arrange for the target vehicle to run into them; survival in these circumstances was a matter of good luck and judgement. In some sectors, where a road was under observation by the enemy, a prominent notice was erected and hessian screens put in place to at least interfere with the enemy's target acquisition. Even this well-intentioned installation was, on at least one occasion, the site of a speed trap set up by the military police – a case of go slow and get hit, or speed up and be reported for speeding. A driver known for his most cautious driving was caught by a speed trap, but his reputation as a very careful driver was enough to save him from being penalised. Apparently, questions were raised in Parliament on the issue of speed traps in France and their adding to the pressures on active service drivers. The almost total lack of speedometers in the BEF's lorry fleet and the general inaccuracy of the Provost timing methods were a part of the driver's daily worries, not to mention shot and shell.

The roads were used by ambulances, staff cars and motor cycle despatch riders as well as the ubiquitous lorry, all travelling at different speeds. By reading his copy of 'Field Service Regulations FSR.1914' junior officers would discover that the lorry was allowed up to 10 mph, buses up to 12 mph and cars/ambulances up to 20 mph. Every facet of active service was covered by FSR, even down to the weight of a watch (4oz) and that of a prismatic compass complete with case (8oz).

We leave to the reader to consider what his or her actions would have been in the same circumstances. In an attempt to reduce dust, experiments took place to redirect the exhaust gases of motor vehicles. Some manufacturers arranged the exhaust pipe to point directly at the road surface but in dry weather this was a perfect mechanism to produce dust. Others discharged the exhaust on the right hand (driver's) side of the vehicle. As all BEF motor vehicles were driven on the 'wrong side' of the road this resulted in discharging the exhaust directly onto any marching troops or passers-by. A blast of dust and exhaust gas would not have been conducive to the fostering of the spirit of comradeship in the BEF, more likely to bring forth certain phrases which we cannot discuss here.

The Battle of the Somme

During February 1916, the by now well-known utility and carrying capacity of the bus resulted in the formation of the 18th Auxiliary Omnibus Company, also known as 588 Coy ASC, with Captain H. Leavis in command. In one of the many twists and turns of war, the company was issued with Locomobiles of American manufacture. The buses had been destined for Germany, but the Royal Navy had other ideas; captured in style on the high seas, the Locomobiles were 'diverted' to France and delivered into the welcoming arms of the ASC. As a mark of respect/disrespect depending on which side of no man's land one occupied, 588 Coy adorned all their new buses with a depiction of the Iron Cross. By that time five Auxiliary Omnibus Companies had been formed and, before long, the preparations for the Battle of the Somme were put in hand.

As the spring of 1916 began to give way to early summer, Anglo-French plans were afoot to deliver a shattering blow to the invader in Picardy. So violent and overwhelming would be the blow that he would have no option but to depart from the 'Sacred Soil of France'.

Wolseley lorries return from Guillemont, Somme 1916.

Designed for use on city streets or gentle ambles along country lanes and safely tucked up in a garage every night, the buses found themselves and their drivers in use twenty-four hours per day, fully or even over loaded, with troops and equipment, crawling in low gear over the deeply rutted roads. Due to the workload and a shortage of drivers, the buses had to be assigned with a single driver instead of the normal complement of two. In effect one driver slept at the company HQ while his opposite number negotiated his bus across the extremely congested Fourth Army area. Before long, the strain on both buses and drivers began to manifest itself with more frequent mechanical breakdowns of the buses and the dire effects of prolonged sleeplessness which afflicted the drivers. However, the ASC carried on to their utmost and seemingly beyond, it being an article of faith not, in any circumstances, to let the infantry down.

The plans changed because of increased enemy pressure on the fortified Verdun sector, which was of national importance to the French; should Verdun have fallen, the French Government would likely have

ASC lorry convoy.

followed it. French troops were diverted from the Somme to be rushed eastwards at whatever the cost to stem the tide of the invader. The BEF found itself taking a larger share of the forthcoming offensive, together with the bringing forward of the date of commencement, as the French found themselves in extreme difficulties at Verdun.

The length of the Somme battle front reached 18 miles, mostly in the area of Sir Henry Rawlinson's Fourth Army with elements of Third Army operating in the north around the village of Gommecourt. On the Somme sector alone, some 500,000 troops had to be supplied with war-like stores, food and in some cases even water, which was supplied in petrol tins giving a most distinct flavour to the British soldier's beloved 'char', a word borrowed from Hindustani meaning tea. Up to late 1916, the railway had to run two water trains daily between the villages of Candas and Canaples, north of Amiens, to augment the water supply for the Somme offensive. So precious was the water supply on the Somme in those quiet times before the battle, the British Tommy could find himself sharing the same water pump with his opposite number in the German army. An unwritten agreement was in force forbidding the firing of shots or the taking of prisoners.

The prodigious build-up of supplies of all kinds strained the ASC to its limits, as well as over-stretching the already creaking French railway system. The Commander-in-Chief of the BEF, Sir Douglas Haig, had already sent urgent requests to London asking for locomotives, engine drivers, railway trucks, vans, coal and extra supplies of new sleepers and rails to replace those worn out by the heavy and ever-increasing traffic loads. Other problems affecting the railway included a shortage of local coal due to the loss of the French coalfields to the enemy; that which was available was often of poor steaming quality. The worn-out locomotives that were no longer capable of hauling a full rake of forty-

French lorry driver.

seven waggons, led to a further load reduction down to thirty-five to forty trucks that was already in place on tracks with steep gradients, as much more of the poor-quality coal was burnt in efforts to coax the worn, tour-expired engines over the higher lines. These circumstances lead to a much-increased work load for MT as the Heads of Steel were some distance from the area of the coming battle.

With the onset of the battle came the creeping problem of supply to the guns and the forward troops. The difficulties reached all the way back to the French Channel ports which lacked the unloading capacity to feed the urgently required war materials to the battle fronts. Warehouses became clogged for lack of trains and indented stores could not be extracted as they lay buried under later consignments. In a most important development for the BEF, Haig urgently requested that a man of experience should be sent out to France to co-ordinate the entire BEF transportation system. This was at the time when the

ASC licence.

Battle of the Somme was raging at maximum effort and the man called forth was Eric Geddes. Geddes was a professional railwayman from the North Eastern Railway which due to his methods charged the lowest fares and freight rates, yet paid the highest dividends of all the railway companies operating in the UK.

Geddes had already gained valuable experience as he was seconded to Lloyd George at the Ministry of Munitions, where his knowledge as one of the leading experts in the use of statistics to forecast traffic requirements, were applied to production and movement of munitions. Haig himself smoothed the path for Geddes when he arrived in France in late August 1916, as he (Haig) had come to realise that putting the best people into roles in which they had excelled in civilian life would work far better for the war effort. Geddes was appointed to the rank of major general and given the title of Director General of Transportation, the first person to have overall control of the entire BEF transportation system, though he was not without his detractors. Reporting to Lloyd George, the military attaché to the Paris embassy informed the Prime Minister thus:

> *You seem to have fluttered the military dovecotes by this unconventional appointment, and it appears to me that there*

is some feeling on the subject, although I should doubt that it is shared by General Haig. You can never get over military prejudices. The appointment of anybody who does not belong to the Military Trade Union is as welcome to soldiers, as the appointment of a bishop drawn from the ranks of stockbrokers would be to the clergy.

Haig did a great deal of work behind the scenes to smooth the feelings of those who felt threatened by the arrival of Geddes and it was to the credit of all, how soon improvements were put in place. Geddes quickly set to work, taking the view that the entire system must work as one and no part could work in isolation. Ships, docks, warehouses, inland waterways, railways and road transport must all work as one machine, each part supplementing and supporting the others. Railway trucks and waggons were discovered in semi-abandoned states, languishing in half-forgotten sidings. Many had been left waiting for labour to unload them which never appeared, others which had broken down had been cut out of the train to await repair with the same result. Urgently required supplies were effectively lost due to breaks in the paper trail that should have accompanied every railway vehicle. All that would change for the better with the arrival of Geddes who soon knew the location of every locomotive, van and waggon and, whether empty or loaded. The same methods were applied to MT and HT, useful loads, mileage, fuel consumption and availability, all were recorded, and a picture built up that predicted bottlenecks and wastage. In particular the worn-out condition of the roads was noted and plans set in motion to rectify the situation.

Haig also asked for more service personnel to be formed into road building and maintenance companies, hoping that by doing so, he would be able to disband the 650-strong gang of Belgian civilian road men '*who cost a great deal of money*'. Haig got his extra road men but, the Belgians were still there months later; they cost money, but they were very good road workers.

The bulkiest loads were fodder, the heaviest, artillery ammunition. Consumption of artillery rounds reached previously unheard of levels for the Somme; over a million rounds being fired prior to the opening of the offensive. On average each division in the line

ASC engaged in troop movement, 1916.

would consume 1,934 tons of ammunition per day of heavy fighting as follows:

Heavy ammunition, 6" and upwards – 500 tons
Medium ammunition, 4.7" and 60pdr – 88 tons
Light Gun ammunition – 450 tons
Small arms and trench ammunition – 176 tons
Royal Engineers stores – 270 tons
Road stone – 400 tons
Rations and Ordnance stores – 270 tons

In all, Fourth Army had the use of 1,200-1,300 lorries employed on ammunition supply per day. The wear on the already somewhat makeshift road system began to accumulate at an alarming rate. In an effort to reduce traffic congestion and wear on the roads, the Army

introduced a one-way system which at least avoided the problems of
lorries trying to squeeze by one another and as a consequence destroying
the soft road edges or, blocking the route completely when, as they had
been doing, keeling over and unable to move while awaiting rescue.
Also, experience revealed that the lorries could not be left on roadsides
when not in use as they caused congestion and were also liable to have
parts or accessories such as lamps removed by passing opportunists.
The solution proved to be the building of hard-standing areas where
the lorries were kept off the roads and under guard. As with all things
in war, this had a knock-on effect, more road stone was required which
had to be conveyed over a long distance by rail and as we now know
the railways were already struggling to deliver the daily requirements.
The lorry, seen as the solution, now added to the problem. Many lamps
would have burned late as frantic staff officers searched for an answer
to the problem of ever larger amounts of supplies passing through a
transport system in which cracks were appearing.

Due to the precarious road system, large quantities of the supplies
that were carried involved what is known as 'dead mileage', that is,
non-revenue earning miles to civilians. Colonel Henniker tells us of
lorries travelling from Franvillers to Edge Hill, a distance of 7 miles,

*ASC lorries
at 'Heads of
Steel' 1916.*

carried a useful load for 2 miles before returning 8 miles to the depot. A 17-mile run for a 2-mile delivery. The colonel also recorded a 40-mile run for a 5- or 6-mile delivery. It can be argued that miles run and price have no value or meaning in a war situation, but in response it must be stressed that transport is the lifeline of an army. It was in 1914-18 and it is today; let us remind ourselves of the enormous lengths the British Army in Afghanistan in the twenty-first century, went to in keeping the forward bases supplied – lives were lost and soldiers horribly maimed, but the supplies had to keep moving. It is one of the unchanging facets of wars ancient and modern. As Sun Tzu reminded his readers, war is an expensive business; the cost of keeping a private soldier on the Western Front was £5 to £6 per week, equal to £295/£353 in today's value.

From the build-up prior to the battle, the commencement and the 148 days of battle that the Army endured, the ASC worked day and night moving up engineers' stores, water, ammunition and food. Due to the inadequate numbers of ambulances provided to deal with the calamitous number of casualties, the ASC drivers found themselves once more bringing in wounded on their return journeys. The lorry was not an ideal means to transport injured and traumatised men but there was no alternative. MT once again proved its worth by instantly switching roles in an emergency.

Large numbers of horses were also killed as A.M. Beatson discovered when taking up supplies. He came across a wooden grave marker inscribed *'To the memory of my dumb pal, Queenie. Killed in action, July 6th, 1916.'*

A typical War Horse, like 'Queenie'? (unknown source)

A.M. Beatson ASC also described a scene where the artillery were in constant action:

Here a battery of ugly howitzers is loosing off salvoes into the Hun trenches, and a little further along a 6-inch gun belched forth a sheet of flame, as with a deafening roar it throws a projectile weighing a hundred pounds screeching through the air to explode several miles behind the German lines. Guns of every size from the 13-pounders to 12- and 15- inch naval guns can be seen and heard pounding away at the enemy. No one appears to pay any attention to these deafening distractions. Adaptability to circumstances and surroundings is a cardinal principle of war. It is amongst such scenes that the Army Service Corps motor-lorries roll up as usual with their loads of rations for the personnel and horses of the guns. A little way behind a battery it will be noted, is the improvised mess of the gunner officers, here you will meet these priceless desperadoes discussing direct hits that have been accorded to their guns, narrow escapes, Grannies, Crumps, Whizz-bangs

20 horse power, Daimler wagonette.

and Heavies. They are totally unconcerned with the dangers that are constantly lurking around; thus, does familiarity breed contempt of even death itself.

The *Wipers Times* published the following dark humour, tongue-in-cheek, infantryman's view of the efforts of his gunner comrades; no doubt the gunners would have replied to refute these 'unfounded' remarks:

Gunners are a race apart, hard of head and hard of heart.
Like the gods they sit, and view, all that other people do
Like the Sisters Three of Fate, they do not discriminate
Our support lines or the Hun's, what's the difference to the guns?
If retaliation you seek? Ring them up and wait a week!
They will certainly reply, in the distant by and by
Should a shell explode amiss, each will swear it was not his
For he's never, never shot, anywhere about that spot
And what is more, his guns could not.

Vicar preaching to some of the troops. (Courtesy of R. Pullen)

Luck plays a large part in the likelihood of an individual surviving a war, the capricious fates could strike without warning as described below:

> *One afternoon I went out with the convoy and delivered the supplies, as usual, to the cavalry who were still bivouacking in the fields around Albert. Returning to Albert, we stopped for two or three minutes to pick up some men on our empty lorries. They were carrying their rifles and packs, and being bound for the same place as us, they naturally got a lift. As matters turned out, it was rather fortunate that the convoy did halt these few minutes; the slight delay probably saved us. We proceeded on our journey, and when about a kilometre short of Albert there was a terrific crash, and the town was hidden from view by a huge black cloud of smoke and dust.*

The above account has all the hallmarks of a 'heavy' shell burst. To this day, there are locations on the Somme that still contain the craters formed by these shells, some 15ft deep and 20-30ft in diameter. The explosion would also propel at high velocity, shell splinters, soil, chalk and flints. Woe unto anyone caught in the radius of the blast. Finding

Troops returning from the line in Wolseley lorries.

themselves plunged into the maelstrom of shellfire that industrial societies could produce, soldiers of all sides quickly developed a sense of how far an incoming round would travel – short fall, on target (me) or a 'goer' (overshoot). Not to make light of such matters and in the true style of soldiers' dark humour the *Wipers Times* offered the following:

> *Hauptmann Van Horner sat in a trench corner*
> *When he heard what he thought was a 'goer'*
> *But he was mistaken*
> *Said Carl Von Haken 'I'll write to his widow; I know 'er.'*

To go some way in clearing confusion regarding the various roles of ASC companies: omnibus companies were also equipped with lorries that could be fitted with seats when required. Petrol companies also carried out more general transport tasks. The 20th Auxiliary Petrol Company (590 MT Coy) was allotted 'nine charabancs' (cars with seats) for the transportation of wounded from Rouen railway station to hospitals.

Appalling road conditions in Northern France.

As the roads and lanes of the Somme were wearing out, so were the calls for ever more road stone. Stone is virtually none existent on the Somme leading to ever higher calls on the railways to deliver. There were instances of medical units on the Somme who dug up their road stone which had been allotted to stable ambulances, loaded same onto lorries and took it with them to their new location. The shortage of stone is still evident in the area today when the visitor to the Somme can see path edges made from empty 18 pounder shells which were far easier to find than natural stone.

Road deterioration accelerated rapidly, so did the lorries and their drivers who were suffering badly due to the very long hours at the wheel often spent under fire. Petrol usage had increased dramatically as the Battle of the Somme progressed so placing yet more demands on the transport system: petrol was being consumed to deliver petrol and so the cycle went on. The design of the lorry at that time was also the root cause of road deterioration. The lorry ran on solid tyres, so the full shock of uneven surfaces was transmitted upwards into the vehicle; to withstand these shocks the vehicles had to be heavily constructed, which in turn multiplied the shocks to the road surface in a never-ending cycle of ruin. The demands on MT grew daily, for example, motor ambulances were in constant use and even though the ambulance had priority, the roads were often blocked by broken-down vehicles or enemy action.

The road between the villages of Fricourt and Mametz was recalled by Major General Anderson:

I think that the memory that comes back more than anything to those of us who remember that old bit of road between Fricourt and Mametz in late 1916. That road was occupied by a stream of traffic day and night. The road never had a bottom to it before the War, and as the lorries went along the road in an endless stream, parties of men threw some stones down between each lorry as they came along. Those who remember will certainly appreciate the importance of transportation.

Mention was also made of the infamous arrow-straight road that runs for 12 miles between Albert and Bapaume:

Perhaps the worst road in France at any time from the beginning to the end of the war was the Albert-Bapaume road after the German retreat to the Hindenburg line. That was terrible. One sent out one's lorry drivers for a trip of 9 miles out and 9 miles back with thirty-six hours' rations on them, because you could never be sure that they would get back in less than that time.

Colonel Taylor added, perhaps with a sense of regret:

Had we known as much about transportation in the Spring of 1916 as we know now, we might have appreciated the situation as follows. We may blow the enemy clean out of sight, but if we do, we won't be able to follow up our success by an advance which would give us material advantage. We can gain a moral advantage and that alone.

It was an allusion to the almost impossible task of moving any form of wheeled transport forward following massive artillery bombardments which, if a road had existed before the bombardments and counter bombardments, it usually didn't later on. Calculations made at the time, concluded that an active, 12-mile sector of the Somme front required 20,000 tons of supplies on a daily basis or, 6,666 3-ton lorry loads to

Troop transport by Daimler, 1916.

sustain the fighting. The sheer magnitude of road traffic was revealed in a census taken over a 24-hour period between 21 and 22 July 1916 at Fricourt. Lyn MacDonald in her book *Somme* relates that the census-takers were forced to wear goggles as the enemy was drenching the road with tear gas, plus, the huge volumes of chalk dust thrown up by the traffic were offering a tempting target for the enemy's artillery. Traffic volumes recorded as follows:

Troops 26,536 • light cars 568 • motor cycles 617 • MT lorries 813 • 6-horse waggons 1,458 • 4-horse waggons 568 • 2-horse waggons 1,215 • 1-horse carts 515 • riding horses 5,404 • motor ambulances 333 • cycles 1,643

MacDonald also reminds us that the number of troops passing the census point exceeded the total British force sent to the Crimean War. The Great War, as it was always referred to until the Second World War, was an undertaking of vast numbers and amounts of everything from men, shirts, rabbit skins, aircraft, ships, tanks, broken glass, horse hoof clippings and a myriad of others, all of which would eventually be carried by MT. For a full listing of men and materials carried see *Statistics of the Military Effort of the British Empire During the Great War.*

As for the BEF's responsibility for roads, this would reach 4,000 miles, for the upkeep of which required 3,370 tons of road stone per day and 40,000 men. The roads were to be built and or maintained to a width of 18ft or 25ft. Roads of both these widths can still be found today in many parts of the old BEF sector of the Western Front. In 'ordinary' traffic conditions, each 25ft road required 100 tons of material per mile, per fortnight. An interesting observation made by a junior officer circa 1915 noted that *'we never see a steam roller at work on the cut-up roads'*. For the benefit of younger readers, road rollers powered by steam were still in use in the 1950s. At the end of that decade several forlorn and sadly neglected steamers were observed in a scrap yard in County Durham. Many more, along with numerous traction engines, could also be seen in a yard south of Stratford-upon-Avon.

The shortage of steam rollers on the BEF's roads was to change very quickly for the better. Enter one Henry Percy Maybury; born in Shrewsbury in 1864, Maybury became an accomplished civil engineer.

'Invicta' road roller in serious trouble.

In 1903 he was appointed engineer and surveyor to Kent where he conducted experiments into dust suppression following the raising of the national speed limit to 20 mph in 1903. A scheme to upgrade Britain's roads was instigated in 1913 and Henry Maybury was appointed Chief Engineering Officer.

The declaration of war in 1914 cut short the scheme and by mid-1916, with trouble brewing with the BEF's transport system, Maybury was despatched to France to confer with GHQ on the provision of roads. The outcome was that he was given responsibility for organising an engineering road service within the BEF and also the provision of road stone.

Steam rollers, as Henry Maybury shortly discovered, were very rare indeed in the BEF's sector of the Western Front. Rollers were urgently needed and in a dashing can-do, press gang-type plan, the UK was scoured for steam rollers and where possible men who knew how to handle them. Unlike the efficient, but shall we say heartless, diesel-powered roller, the steamer needed someone who was familiar with all the little foibles of very individual engines. Most would only work efficiently when roller and driver worked as one, hence the long-held practice of one driver only being allotted to a particular engine. The collection of steam rollers grew fast, but so did the complaints of counties left bereft of any rollers to maintain their own road surfaces. But the war had to be won and the humble roller with a boiling heart of iron was needed as much as was a 15-inch gun. The image shows an Aveling-Porter roller in dire straits on the Western Front, probably a victim of the infamous 'soft edges' of many of the roads.

Henry Maybury, Road Engineer.

An example of the desperate condition of the roads was given by John Bagot Glubb in his memoir *Into Battle* for 7-17 October 1916:

> *The 50th Division are going out to rest, but the gunners and sappers will stay in the line. We extended the tramline back from High Wood to Bazentin-le-Petit, to relieve the road. The roads in the forward area are becoming incredibly bad. They were originally required in a tremendous hurry on 15th September, behind the advancing infantry, and so the shell holes were filled with any old rubbish. Bricks from ruined villages are the best material, but sometimes bits of wood or logs were used, earth, dead horses, or even human corpses.*

These roads quickly became impassable, waggons on the Mametz to Bazentin-le-Petit road constantly sank up to their axles and in doing so, completely blocked the road.

As a priority, Geddes, now with overall responsibility for the BEF's transport, insisted on the expansion of the narrow-gauge, light railway systems. New lines were built and existing lines were, where possible,

HT casualty evacuation, artist's impression – Mike O'Brien.

quickly expanded. The new lines required less road stone than a road and could be built very quickly. Due to the by now semi-static nature of the Somme fighting, the larger, heavy calibre guns with their long ranges did not need constant shifting forward, making them ideal for ammunition deliveries by light railway. The Somme area became populated with marshalling yards and lines reaching far out on to the battlefield. Today's visitor can catch glimpses of light railway track in field boundary fences, mute testament to the massive endeavours of the BEF over 100 years ago. The worn out and damaged lorries, relieved by the expanded light railways, were taken into workshops and, where humanly possible, restored to as new or even better condition. The same could be said of the roads as the constant pounding of heavy vehicles was at last reduced and to some extent, more permanent repairs took place.

The Battle of the Somme petered out around 19 November 1916, when the 19th (Western) Division was withdrawn from a position in front of Grandcourt. Although the battle was over, the area was still an extremely dangerous place as the crew of a lorry carrying wounded discovered. Shells were falling intermittently leading the driver to push on as fast as the '*shocking road would allow*'. Unfortunately, a large shell

ASC Scrap Yard, 1917.

hole had appeared leaving the driver no option but to slowly manoeuvre around the obstacle without becoming 'bogged' in the porridge-like wet spoil thrown out by the explosion. Suddenly there came the harrowing shriek of an on-rushing shell bent on destruction. The survivor of the blast that followed reported:

> *Heaven and Earth became mixed together accompanied by an acrid smell and then, silence. The lorry had been damaged and enveloped in a thick cloud of evil smelling smoke which gradually drifted away.*

Finding himself dazed but otherwise unhurt, the survivor looked to his mate who had been driving – he was dead, slumped over the steering wheel. Another man who had been in the cab was also dead. The only thing that now mattered was to get away from the site as quickly as the damaged lorry would allow. With the two dead men still in the cab, he managed to move the corpse of the driver across the seat then took the controls himself. Fortunately, he got the lorry clear a few seconds before another shell exploded with a terrific shriek and roar exactly where the lorry had been stopped when the first shell detonated. Driving erratically due to shock, he reached a dressing station where he was later told the staff could barely understand him. As for the wounded being conveyed in the lorry, he could not bring himself to enquire if any had survived the blast.

In the spring of 1917, an ASC unit moving forward following the retreat of the invader to the east of Peronne came across the sad landscapes of deliberately destroyed villages. Even the cemeteries had been desecrated by the removal of corpses from coffins. The Germans had used the lead shells to bury their own dead. A Frenchman who had lived in a village under occupation had been told by German soldiers that their orders were to destroy fruit trees, gardens, graves and houses, in order to cause a revolt by the civil population who, it was hoped, would instigate demands for peace terms with the enemy. These words had been penned by an ASC officer who did not seem to have any personal dislike for the German soldier, only that soldier's militaristic government and, as reported later in this work, the Germans were employing the same methods in 1918.

As with all of the battles on the Western Front, salvage was a key part of the ASC workload. According to A.M. Beatson, huge amounts of taxpayer's property would be left behind including shells, small arms and their ammunition, soldier's equipment and clothing, rations, grenades and occasionally, rum. The dead bodies of soldiers were also recovered and taken to the nearest military cemetery. If it was possible, an officer of the Graves Registration Committee would identify the corpse, whether British or German, before burial by an army padre. The salvaged *matériel* was then sent back to bases for sorting into that which could be re-used or written off and sold for cash.

Beatson tells us of the farmers returning to the sites of the villages of Beaumont Hamel and Serre which only months before had been virtually wiped off the map. Some of the returnees also began to search the devastated landscape for money that they had buried in the face of the German advances of 1914. Beatson again: '*Alas! I fear they seldom if ever find it.*' But should their crops prosper, the BEF would provide reaping and threshing machines. The ASC recovered salvage of enormous value and the farmers risked their lives – many were killed when the plough struck ammunition – as they sought to bring 'the bread basket of France' back into production.

The curé of a village church in the devastated area of the Somme, was given permission by Fourth Army to travel to his church to recover any sacred items that might have survived. It soon became apparent that the church, the curé's house and the village had been wiped off the map; he had spent forty years in the village but could find not a single item that might relate to human occupation. Brigadier General Ludlow also visited the battlefield to search for the grave of his son, Stratford Walter. The search proved unsuccessful (Stratford's remains were recovered in 1930). Viewing the devastation, the general remarked that six villages were now only names on a map *'as there is nothing to denote that they have ever been occupied as human habitations'*. As he searched for his son, the general noted the huge amounts of salvage waiting to be cleared, *'coats, tunics, rifles, bayonets, bully beef tins unopened, shells, grenades and unopened boxes of grenades, skulls, bones and shrapnel helmets lay in all directions'*.

The normality of farm life and food production would be disrupted again on two occasions in 1918. The two villages – Serre and Beaumont Hamel – were lost when the BEF retreated in the face of the German Spring Offensive of that year, only for the BEF to advance westwards a few months later and reclaim the lost villages. A mere twenty-two years were to pass before the German army appeared again, this time to stay for five dark years.

As a footnote to the Battle of the Somme, railway staff officer Colonel Mance summed up the logistic problem bedevilling the BEF:

> In those early days transport was all right so long as the weather was dry because MT kept to the roads and HT went alongside the roads over fields. But the moment there was any rain, the whole supply was stopped because HT had to come on to the roads and the roads could not carry it.

Thanks to Geddes, who had to move very quickly, in a very short time most of the supply problems were solved.

Chapter 7

Maintaining Order on the Road System

Free for alls, where drivers have no regard at all for themselves or others, have been a menace from the dawn of wheeled vehicles. There is a theory based on bone damage, that the pharaoh Tutankhamen may have fallen from a speeding chariot, subsequently dying from his injuries in a 'road accident'. Street accidents involving horse drawn vehicles were common well before the advent of the motor vehicle as emergency stops could not be made.

The Western Front, with its shortage of roads and vast amount of traffic, human, animal and MT, presented an entirely new problem in policing – to win the war the traffic must flow, and flow in the direction and at the time required. We have seen the result of traffic chaos at Loos when men lost their lives following severe delays on the road. The organisation tasked with traffic control (it must be stressed, not the staff work which should have worked out march times and traffic flows) was 'Provost' an ancient title of European origins which signified one who became the most trusted servant of kings and emperors in all matters of discipline and protocol. Eventually, the numerous duties of the Provost service required extra staff, therefore the title, Provost Marshal came into use to signify the head of the security department. The earliest known reference to Provost in service with the English Crown was William of Cassingham who was appointed by King Henry III on 28 May 1241. By the year 1312, royal instruction defined the duties of the Provost Marshal thus: *'Jurisdiction, which is even more potent and terrible than all of the evil omens and witchcraft.'*

In 1662, Francis Markham added:

The Provost Marshal should love justice, be impartial and have an eye that can gaze on all objects without winking, while having a heart filled with discreet compassion and not touched by foolish or melting pity.

Quite a modern outlook? Finally, in 1809, Arthur Wellesley, later the Duke of Wellington, called for a regular provost establishment to be attached to armies sent abroad. The following year, 1810, Wellesley added that only professional soldiers should be used for provost services as up to that time it had been a largely civilian role. The ranks of PM Provost Marshal, APM Assistant Provost Marshal, DAPM Deputy Assistant Provost Marshal, MP Military Police, MMP Mounted Military Police, would become familiar to all ranks of the BEF. An incident occurred at the Battle of Loos in which an MP stopped 72 Brigade because the brigadier general in command was not in possession of a pass to enter the battle area…the brigadier was at the head of approximately 4,000 heavily armed men plus his small, personal staff. A case for reading the words of Francis Markham?

On the subject of Assistant Provost Marshal, the *Wipers Times* informed its wide readership that APM actually stood for '*A permanent malingerer*'. A printer's error, surely? Those lonely figures who stood out in all weathers on road junctions, bridges and level crossings, waving a red 'stop' lantern were not intended to be an instrument of suffering for oncoming drivers. He kept his vigil to enforce the will of the commander-in-chief, defined as keeping the traffic moving as safely and efficiently as possible. Largely unloved by their comrades, Provost had a long history of service to the Crown. Now they found themselves dealing with a war on wheels in which heavy vehicles with rudimentary brakes, demanded passage by day and by night, no allowances being made for weather or broken-down vehicles, the traffic must flow. As the war progressed the lorries would often be carrying infantrymen who were only too pleased to save their weary legs. When buses were available they would also be thrown into the traffic mix. For all this to work rules had to be established for the safety of the soldiers and to ensure that the traffic flowed, delivering, men, munitions and food.

As previously mentioned, road circuits were established which in effect were one-way systems. It is still possible to this day to drive on a BEF Road Circuit. The map shown is that of the circuit on a part of the Somme battlefield. These circuits were taken very seriously to the point that a military policeman recalled being instructed as follows: '*If you sees 'aig* [Sir Douglas Haig] *going against the circuit, book 'im.*'

To understand and use the circuits, the driver had to be aware of many variables. He had to have a map of the circuit mounted in a prominent place within his cab. Some roads were closed altogether

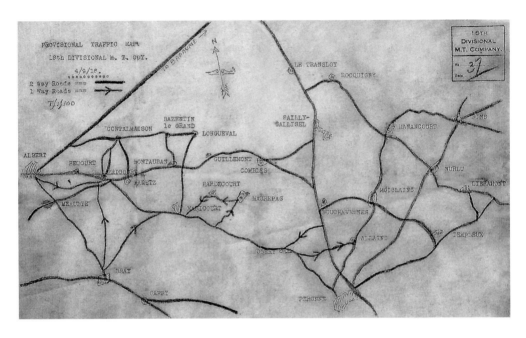

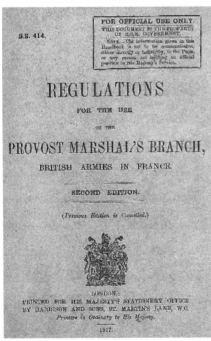

S.S. 414, 1917.

to save wear and tear. Roads coloured red upon the map were usually designated two-way but, be aware of local differences. Blue roads might be used by light traffic in both directions but, heavy traffic was to proceed only in the direction of the arrows on the map. Roads not showing any colour were not to be used by steam engines, buses or heavy lorries. Horses could not be exercised on coloured roads and ambulances had special routes shown by dotted red or blue lines. It was quite complex and in darkness or fog and without lighting, it would be an easy matter for a driver to lose direction and take a wrong turn. However, Second Army Traffic Orders of January 1917 reminds MPs that: *'The regulation of traffic so as to prevent obstruction or accident requires tact. Never get flustered or annoyed.'*

S.S. 414 also of 1917 gave the following advice to MPs through a comprehensive training course:

Principles of Traffic Control

Why is traffic control necessary? Why it will only work properly if everyone plays his part, particularly the drivers of lorries, is on account of:

1. *We are fighting on a narrow front with increasing depth*
2. *Few roads fit for heavy traffic particularly lorries*
3. *Few roads running directly up to the front*
4. *The many varieties of traffic*
5. *In wet weather roads become impassable*
6. *Roads so narrow*
7. *Always a sprinkling of new drivers*

Efficient Traffic Controls

These must be obeyed, as they operate directly under a Provost Marshal. They enforce the traffic, i.e. refuse certain roads, disentangle muddles, control speed, see that rules of the road are observed. Road discipline indicates the state of discipline in the unit. From the senior officer down to the last-joined private it is up to them to help as no system of traffic control will answer if discipline is bad.

The traffic orders also caution against stopping heavily-laden vehicles and restive horses should not be stopped when they were going up or down hills. The MP was also to familiarise himself with the colour codes of flags flown on the cars of officers of various ranks: **Union Flag** – Commander-in-Chief, **Red and Blue** – General Headquarters, **Red flag with Black Cross** – Army Commanders, **Red flag with White Cross** – Corps Commanders, **Red Flag** – Divisional Commanders, **Dark blue, light blue and red flag** – Royal Flying Corps, **Dark blue with red zig-zag** – Artillery Commanders.

LOST, STOLEN OR STRAYED.

— o — o — o —

A Gent's Bicycle

JUST LIKE
THIS ONE :—

Last seen wandering by itself on the main road to Lille.

Answers to the name of "GOVIE" (short for "Government").

No questions asked of anyone who returns same within four weeks.

—o—o—o—

Owner. The Kennels. Cobrieux.

Spoof advertisement for a stolen bike.

Despatch riders were not to be restricted as their work was classed to be of the utmost importance. It came to be realised that lax use of the telephone system had been responsible in some cases for the enemy having prior knowledge of BEF offensive operations so, where possible use of the telephone gave way to the dashing, dust-covered despatch rider, complete with goggles and flapping, long canvas coat with a map case carried around his neck.

Motor cycles found to be in the possession of a unit other than that to which it was allotted, generated paperwork that could find its way upward to divisional and upwards again to corps command. There was a war to be won, but who lost the machine, where is it and how do we get it back? were questions requiring answers. Push bikes were also prime targets for opportunists. The rider had to find someone to mind his bike or potentially find himself responsible and 'on report' if it was gone when he went to retrieve it. In later years, the water at RAF Honiley in Warwickshire developed a strange taste and colour. Investigation revealed that the water tank was almost brim-full of push bikes. They had been 'liberated' after dark from the surrounding district by airmen returning from the local public houses, the bikes being tossed into the tank before reaching the guardhouse.

As for drivers, the same orders stated:

When driving Government vehicles men are 'on duty'. They are not to stop at Estaminets and similar places and leave their vehicles unattended outside. No lorry or 'bus is to pass another lorry or 'bus travelling in the same direction.

When travelling in convoy, every group of six lorries had to be separated by a 25-yard gap. The last lorry in the group had to carry an 18-inch diameter red disc; the last vehicle in the whole convoy carried a double red disc. The discs were provided by arrangements with the individual army commanders. The BEF operated up to five armies on the Western Front; the commander's task carried crushing responsibility and, although he had a staff, their numbers were usually quite small. Signing off requests for red discs when enduring what was known at the time as 'mental crucifixion' when attacks were raging cannot have helped the generals' disposition.

The responsibilities of the Provost service spread even further to include, as laid down in S.S. 414, **'Sanitary Duties,** *to keep a constant watch on the sanitary condition of billets and their surroundings. They will at once report all cases where ground has been fouled, refuse left unburnt, or dead animals have not been removed.'* Street patrols enforced the closing time of bars and shops, stragglers were conducted to their proper billets and suspect persons arrested to *'prevent plundering and the ill treatment of inhabitants'*. Provost Marshals were also reminded that they could, at any time arrest and detain persons who were subject to military law and committing offences. Importantly, Provost Marshals were strictly forbidden to inflict punishments on their own authority.

Finally, it should be remembered that Provost was dealing twenty-four hours per day with heavily armed and very fit men, a good number of whom would have been pumped up with adrenalin. It says much for the unsung Red Caps that they did so largely with tact and understanding and at the same time keeping the traffic moving; some lost their lives while doing so.

Chapter 8

Keeping MT on the Road

It cannot be stressed too highly how the Base Mechanical Transport depots, Advanced Mechanical Transport depots, spare parts supply, maintenance, heavy repair shops, tyre presses and mobile workshops, all played a vital role in keeping the MT moving. The entire system came under the watchful eye of the Director of Transport for the British Armies in France, Major General W.G.B. Boyce. Based in his London office, Major General Boyce, could tell at a glance the whereabouts and condition, of any means of British motorised transport on the Western Front correct to the night before, including vehicles awaiting shipment to France. The American journalist Isaac F. Marcosson, who visited Sir Douglas Haig at GHQ, writes in *Business of War* that '*Boyce could smell a mistake*' and well knew that '*knowledge is power*'.

Due to the lack of pre-war preparations and the speed of the extensions to the Army's commitments, it had been impossible to standardise vehicles. Hence the multiplicity of spare parts carried in the BEF's base depots. The first Base Mechanical Depot was established at the city of Rouen on the River Seine which had unfortunate associations for Anglo-Saxons as the site of the execution of Joan of Arc. By the spring of 1915, as the BEF front lines extended from the North Sea to Picardy, coupled with the rise in MT numbers, it was decided to open another base further north.

The location chosen for the new base to be known as No.2 Base MT Depot, was Calais. Rail journeys eastwards would be shorter from Calais and congestion in the Rouen area significantly eased. The site chosen was that of an abandoned timber yard located on the Quai de l'Est (eastern quay) and bounded by two roads, Rue Descartes and Rue Mollien. A total of eight 10,000 square foot stores plus administrative offices were erected. The main tasks allotted to the Calais depot were the provision of spare parts for all the hundreds of American vehicles arriving every month and serving with the BEF, which greatly simplified the whole process of ordering and despatch of spares. Calais was also maintaining a two-month stock of motor cycles and a two-month stock of pneumatic tyres to serve the needs of First and Second Armies and General Headquarters (GHQ).

When completed, the Calais operation became the Northern Line of Communication and Rouen the Southern Line of Communication. The new depot opened on 1 September 1915 and eventually held a stock of sixteen makes of American and British vehicles. Although it operated on the same site as the base depot, the Advance Mechanical Transport depot was kept separate as it dealt directly with the armies within its zone of operations. The history of the Calais base was written by Lieutenant Colonel, G.C.G. Blunt, published by the *ASC Quarterly*, circa 1920.

The detailed motor repair manual is nothing new; as MT and the demands for spares rapidly increased in volume and variety, it became evident that parts lists supplied by motor manufacturers were often wrong, leading to all sorts of problems as urgently needed vehicles stood idle for want of the correct spares. To overcome this cycle of confusion, a group of experts in the field of MT was tasked with producing a 'vocabulary' of each type and make of vehicle in service with the BEF. This involved the complete dismantling of the vehicle and the measuring and recording of each and every part down to the last split pin and washer. There were those who said the 'vocabulary' could not be done, those who said it would take five years – both were confounded when the task was completed and published in just two years.

Great Britain's oldest ally, Portugal fought on the Western Front and No.2 Base Depot handled all of the MT requirements of the Portuguese. Every item, from a sprocket to a lorry had to be strictly accounted for and duly authorised by the financial administrator of the Portuguese Expeditionary Force. It was all in a day's work, the war was running on two essentials – wheels and paper. Without the ability to trace and record every single transaction, from supplying a complete 'B' Type bus to a washer, the Army could not be supported in the field of operations.

Heavy Repair Shops

Following early problems, these establishments were to become a triumph of skills and organisation, staffed by tradesmen of the highest order, vehicles that to the untutored eye appeared beyond hope of ever making it back on to the road, were very often miraculously transformed to better than new condition. The Heavy Repair Shops were usually located just outside the danger zone of hostile artillery fire. A better description would have been 'Large Motor Vehicle Factories' as that is how the shops worked, employing hundreds of skilled men and women. Local French women were glad of well-paid jobs while their husbands and sons were away fighting. It is known that by 1917, women of Queen Mary's Army Auxiliary Corps were undertaking various roles in heavy repair shops replacing men who were sent to the fighting arms. The women were not, as is sometimes noted, sent to the front lines.

The raw material for the shops was provided by the Casualty Park, a sight to send shivers down the spine of even battle-hardened soldiers. Here was graphic evidence that the work of the supply services was not a 'cushy number' with the mangled, blood spattered wrecks of lorries and staff cars, ambulances riven by shrapnel bullets and, the almost unrecognisable remains of a despatch rider's motor cycle, bearing silent testament to the crushing power of industrialised war. The Casualty Parks were supposed to be screened from view by passing traffic so as to prevent the morale of all ranks becoming

Ford Model 'T' ambulances undergoing maintenance.

damaged by the sight of the gruesome remains. I.F. Marcosson put it succinctly when describing the scene, '*It is precisely like the effect on a man who has to pass through a morgue on the way to the operating theatre.*'

Every vehicle casualty was first examined as to the probability of its ever returning to service. Should the vehicle fail inspection, any components that were still able to function were removed by a 'Retrieving Section' and sent to the stores. Metals were sorted into ferrous and non-ferrous, much of the total being melted down on site to be used again. German prisoners were also employed on salvage work, which they did on a voluntary basis. Vehicles that passed into the shop were dismantled and every component was cleaned and examined. Cracked or bent chassis were put in the hands of specialists who repaired and straightened them. Engines were removed, stripped down and thoroughly checked for wear and damage. When finally re-assembled, the engines were placed on a test rig and started up to test for leaks and, most importantly, power output. The 3-ton lorry was rated at 40 horse power (HP) and should the HP not come up to specification, the engine was returned to the shop for investigation; only when it performed properly was it allowed to proceed further. The (mostly wooden) bodies were placed in the hands of coachbuilders for repair and overhaul to as-new condition, plus any modifications required.

When all was ready the vehicle was handed over to the Test Branch Mechanical Transport, an entirely independent organisation that thoroughly tested and inspected the vehicle as to whether it was fit to proceed to service or be returned to shop. A total of five Heavy Repair Shops were established, at Rouen, Paris and Le Havre.

Life in a Heavy Repair Shop

By great good fortune, a war diary of a heavy repair shop has survived. What follows is an edited version of **319 MT Company ASC (Heavy Repair Shop)** which was formed in March 1915 and initially based in Paris. Due to reasons of repetition and space, the diary is not reproduced in full. Where possible, the words and punctuation are as written over 100 years ago.

The full text of the diary can be found in the UK National Archives; WO95/4166 (Lines of Communication)

1915

24 October: Discipline in the shop not what it should be – had this seen to. Fatigue parties put to work in gangs under an NCO; 2 men detailed for cleaning up each shop daily.

25 October: 2 De Dion lorries delivered – arranged that the drivers instruct our own men.

29 October: Major General Landon, Deputy Director of Transportation inspected the workshops, looked at O.K. lorries and found defects – lubricators not repaired – nuts and bolts not properly washered and many needing attention by 'Wheelers' – not very large items but sufficient to cause larger faults later on.

1 November: Lorries that should have been ready for convoy not finished. Some that had to be re-painted, not finished, also to be washed – should have been done before but due to slackness of NCO in charge it was omitted to be done – extra painters procured to start early tomorrow (6.30am)

Removing useful spares from damaged vehicles. (Courtesy of R. Pullen)

5 November: Lorry caught fire through men smoking – no material damage done – Cpl. Boden acted with great promptitude and coolness to put the fire out.

11 November: Owing to lack of clerical assistance & stress, stocktaking is impossible – materials and tools moved out & no receipts issued – parts and materials issued to shop and only roughly accounted for.

(Just prior to August 1914, officers were held financially responsible for stock shortages. An old adage advised: 'if you must lose anything, make it something worth £20,000, they can't stop that from your pay' – £20,000 being equal to £1,000,000 today.)

13 November: Several lorries ready for service found to have wrong size tyres fitted.

19 November: DDT [Director General of Transport] *wants cabs of lorries to be made as weather proof as possible.*

23 November: Thornycroft lorry caught fire – no major damage – caused through backfire into the carburettor.

12 December: Trouble with lorries – Drivers caused more trouble than the lorries, they are very bad drivers.

A report of the year 1921 mentions issues of lubrication 'in the late war'. It was noted that over use of oils and grease was wasteful and rarely beneficial to the vehicle. It was also deemed *'extremely undesirable that the lubrication of any part of a motor vehicle should be dependent on whether the driver remembers or cares to apply lubricants to the 30 or 40 places required'*.

1916

7 January: Mr. Hutton, manager of Wolseley Motor Company called to see defects in Wolseley lorries – second motion shaft failed in the majority of cases. [gearbox component]. *It seems that the replacement parts sent out from the factory are still held at Base.*

21 February: Wired for more lorry drivers to despatch vehicles to the front.

New Wolseley lorries at the Birmingham factory. (Courtesy of R. Pullen)

25 March: Director of Transport phoned ref. shortage of lorries – I explained that the canvas hoods and frames that 'He' had requested, were taking a long time to make and fit. And last (but not least) up to now we have been repairing the lorries which could be fixed quickly; now we have run out of those and only have those requiring heavy repair left.

4 April: DDT complaint – not satisfied with the way vehicles are tested and inspected before they leave here. Slight adjustments by drivers and visual inspection by an artificer would rectify most of the defects. Nearly all breakdowns are caused by lack of minor adjustments & inexperienced drivers – mechanical defects cannot be avoided.

A note concerning the above remark: *I asked a driver how often he checked the oil levels in the engine of his lorry – his reply was 'when smoke starts coming from the engine, Sir'.*

18 April: D of T [Director of Transport] *phoned: was it possible to get electrically driven machines suitable for mobile workshops based in Paris? Made enquiries everywhere – unobtainable.*

26 April: Electric power plant in the workshop – not sufficient power to run all necessary lights and machines – 2 Westinghouse Representatives to inspect and furnish a report.

October: Placed order for 100 sets of 'Free Skate' anti-skid chains to be supplied at 55FF [French Francs] *per chain.*

October: Visited Dunlop works ref. excessive number of tyres returned to us as 'unrepairable', letter written for an explanation.

October: Visited French stores to obtain solid tyres from French Authorities for use on British Army vehicles.

13 May: Lorries getting roughly treated & generally uncared for – they must be inspected twice a week.

From this point, the words of Lieutenant R.S.M. Sturgess, (who appears to have been the diarist for the above) can be quoted at some length as he recorded his experiences with No.1 Heavy Repair Shop. The full account can be read in WO95/4166.

Lieutenant Sturgess opens his account by reminding us that:

MT is a great part of the modern army and suffers casualties to its vehicles. As Base hospitals were for men, so were Heavy Repair shops for vehicles. The shop was set up to deal with all French & British makes of vehicles; employing 400 skilled men including, fitters, blacksmiths, wheelers, coppersmiths, electricians, spring makers and, frame platers. The various specialised sections include, personnel, vehicle park, body shop, lorry shop, unit shop, machine shop, foundry, testing section and stores.

***The vehicle park**, known as 'casualty park' usually contained 300 dilapidated lorries which arrived by rail. Many show 'open wounds' received in action and other internal troubles due to wear and tear in the battle area.*

***Body shop**, removes and overhauls bodywork and, turns same out like new.*

***Lorry shop**, lorries completely stripped down to the last nut and bolt, everything checked, tested & replaced as necessary.*

THE
RENOWNED
TYLOR
SUBSIDY
ENGINE,

TYPE J.B. 4,
5" BORE, 6" STROKE.

DEVELOPS
45 B.H.P. AT 1,000
R.P.M.

□

J.B. 4 TYPE ENGINE.

10,000 OF THE ABOVE ENGINES
IN WAR SERVICE.

TRIED AND PROVED IN TANKS,
WAR DEPT. SUBSIDY LORRIES,
LIGHT RAILWAY LOCOMOTIVES,
BALLOON WINCHES, ETC.

Send for Catalogue and Particulars.

TYLOR ENGINES

Tylor Subsidy engine.

Unit shop, *engine, gearbox, back axle repairs, all parts steam cleaned and washed.*

Machine shop *carries out any machining required on engines and gearboxes. Electroplates worn parts back to original sizes – saving the expense of buying in new.*

Foundry, *melts scrap metal & turns out spare parts, including cylinder heads, that are in short supply. Fuel burnt is waste oil from lorries being repaired.*

The whole foundry was built out of materials to hand – only one man had any idea how to build a furnace, he was a regular soldier who had been a furnaceman at Aldershot. Castings were produced in aluminium, phosphor-bronze, gunmetal, steel and cast iron. All the patterns and moulds were made in house.

Coppersmith's shop, *mainly repairing damaged radiators.*

Tyre press, *changing solid tyres.*

Lieutenant Sturgess described a remarkable achievement by the foundry regarding a tyre press. These were very heavy machines that pressed solid tyres over the rim of the wheels. One such press broke down when a ¾-ton casting cracked. There were serious concerns raised when it was discovered that a new replacement would take three months to arrive, tyres being almost as important as petrol to MT. Nothing fazed, the foundrymen produced patterns, a mould and scoured the surrounding area for suitable scrap metal. The mix of the metal was crucial to the performance of the finished article as was the temperature of the furnace and the colour of the molten metal. The 'pour' was successful and was repeated as castings in more presses showed cracks appearing. The press in question was back in service in three weeks, far less than the three months required to obtain a new casting. This whole venture was a testament to the range of skills to be found in Great Britain at that time. Sadly, they have now largely disappeared.

Solid tyre press, unknown source.

Magneto repairs *required intricate work to very fine tolerances.*

Testing section*, after final assembly, lorry is test loaded and given an extensive road test and hill climb, followed by final engine tune up before application of final paint finish, tools lamps and lights also attached.*

Cracked chassis*, these were dealt with by local French firm using oxy-acetylene welding carried out by their own skilled men at 'contract' rates.*

White metal*, produced on site for lining engine bearings, casting new pistons for worn engines plus other uses. (White metal is a silver-*

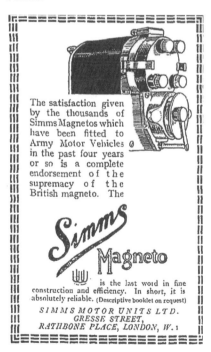

The satisfaction given by the thousands of Simms Magnetos which have been fitted to Army Motor Vehicles in the past four years or so is a complete endorsement of the supremacy of the British magneto. The

Simms **Magneto**

is the last word in fine construction and efficiency. In short, it is absolutely reliable. (Descriptive booklet on request)

SIMMS MOTOR UNITS LTD.
GRESSE STREET,
RATHBONE PLACE, LONDON, W.1

Advertisement for Magneto.

coloured alloy which is easily fusible and suitable for use in high speed bearings.)

Stores *contained 200,000 items – daily issue averaged 1,000.*

Tyres*, pneumatic tyres – repairs and re-treading carried out under contract with the firm of Dunlop. A tyre examiner was employed to assess which tyres were worth repair and forwarding to Paris where Dunlop were operating. (See above, dispute over condition of tyres.)*

Nearly all of the above diary and descriptions of work at 1 Heavy Repair Shop would have been lost to us but for the survival of Lieutenant Sturgess's notes. They clearly demonstrate the complexity and extensive variety of tasks and skills involved to keep MT on the road.

The Mobile Workshop

Yet another example of the ingenuity displayed by the BEF, the mobile workshop, roamed the area traversed by MT. Based on the 5-ton lorry, the fully equipped workshop could rival a small factory in its ability to repair or manufacture damaged or missing components. Machines carried included a lathe, milling machine, bench drill and grinding

Wolseley mobile workshop.

machine, plus a large assortment of hand tools and other equipment of a specialised nature, such as hub extractors. Electrical power for the machines was provided by a separate petrol engine which drove a dynamo. Later, to save space, the lorry's engine was used to drive the dynamo, a practice still in use in the 1960s by travelling showmen. The sides of the lorry lifted upwards to form an awning and a floor extension would be pulled out and supported on folding legs, then the mobile was open to receive clients. A further addition to the services offered by the mobile was the introduction of trailers to carry spare engines. A crane was built into the trailer to allow engine changes at the roadside or hard standing area. Separate stores lorries accompanied the mobiles which also carried clerks to assist the storekeepers.

The mobiles operated in the danger zones, often set up in an open field, the fitters toiled away knowing full well the risks involved from bullets and shells. Shell splinters, ragged chunks of steel travelling at several hundred miles per hour crashing into a lorry or ambulance, could cause myriad problems to the vehicle, not forgetting the driver and his mate who were far more susceptible to shell damage.

The 'client base' of mobiles was composed overwhelmingly from ammunition and supply columns engaged in the never-ending tasks of feeding men and the ever-hungry guns. Despatch riders were also regular clients as they were often thrown from their machines by hitting the many deep, water-filled ruts in the roads. If the rider was lucky, a passing lorry crew would help him to heave the motor cycle on board and ferry him to

'Mountain' of radiators, ASC scrapyard, France.

the nearest mobile where succour awaited. Mobiles were also known to go to the rescue of ditched vehicles. If, after retrieval, the lorry could not be readily made roadworthy it would be towed to a suitable parking place where the mobile crew would set about rectifying the vehicle.

The mobile workshops did have some quiet times during which, one-offs would be manufactured. In at least one instance, the lads produced a 'splendid' wash basin for the commanding officer from scrap aluminium. The same officer was also supplied with a stove and water heater, both made 'in house' and as a matter of routine his office was fitted up with electric lights. Another project involved the making of a christening cup using melted down silverware. Now mostly lost to history, perhaps a little light has been shone upon the mobile pioneers who by their ingenuity and hard work, played a vital role in the story of MT at war.

Life as a Mobile Fitter

More often than not, the mobile fitters were unsung and soon forgotten, it seems the history of wars pays no heed to those who made the whole 'machine' work. The following will go some way to rectifying this omission from history. Entitled, *Somme Battles, Rawlinson's 1V Army 1916,* the hand-written document is anonymous. It is reproduced in part here by kind permission of the Royal Logistics Corps Museum, ref. RLCA 3975 B1.

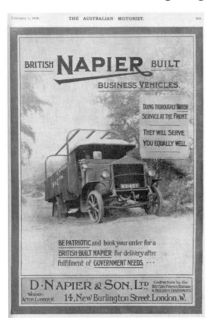

Advertisement for 'Napier' lorry.

'At the commencement of the Somme Battles, 1ˢᵗ July 1916, the artillery shells were carried by M.T. ASC units up to the firing positions of the guns. Guns were also hauled out of their positions by the ASC as the Royal Artillery at that time did not possess their own mechanised transport. Senior NCO fitters and mechanics were sent forward when temporary facilities were established in the field to support MT. It is surprising little mention is made in Artillery or the Corps histories, of the tasks carried out by this group. The officers were changed and moved about so rapidly they had little time for recording much of possible interest of those hectic times.

Following a communal bath taken in an old dye works where a French Lady scrubbed the men without turning a hair, I was whisked off by lorry to join the new group HQ located in a sail cloth covered hollow basin just out of sight of Thiepval on the Somme Battlefield. Until recently, this hollow had been an assembly place for infantry to access the trench system in several directions. In this hollow was our advanced workshop which consisted of a few pieces of timber and more sail cloth. There appeared to be more NCOs than privates, we were certainly in a position to see and hear much enemy activity, for our workshop roof was only just below the line of sight from Thiepval and much activity could be seen. Two petrol dumps had been hit with flames rising to great heights, and also a small arms dump was likewise on fire with ammunition popping off for 3 or 4 days. Machine gun fire could be heard, &, in the afternoons, the enemy artillery would open up with his shells screaming over our heads as they searched for a large shell dump behind us.

One afternoon the shelling had been going on & overshooting their target, we saw roofs and tiles blown into the air in Dernancourt village. *(approx. 2 miles south west of Albert)* Five people were killed & a number wounded. The last shot of the day fell near our hollow & made a crater just outside & the batman to our workshop officer went down into the crater for a souvenir, & picked up the base of the shell, but burnt his fingers & dropped it; it was the size of a dessert plate.

Before the rains came, our formation Commander decided to move his HQ nearer to our location & the shell dump & had two French peasant families turned out of their cottages for his HQ. I believe if I remember correct, two days after establishing his HQ, two enemy shells exploded in the gardens of the cottages, so he returned to his old HQ, but I am stating events in advance of their happenings.

On the day I arrived at this section, I was met by a man who said he would carry my kit to where the NCOs sleep on the ground allotted to them. He advised me to keep out of the Workshop Officer's way in the mornings "as he has got a liver but, he is alright later as the day wears on". However, I reported to the Workshop Officer who I later learned was a mining engineer who had given up his job in South America to join up for the war. Liver trouble or not, he was a practical man & had common sense, a contrast to some of his newly joined fellows. His first words to me were "I understand you have had experience of vehicle inspections, I have a job for you" & picking up a handful of inspection reports, told me to accompany him. We walked towards the shell dump, where groups of lorries were standing. Where he remarked, "Now, I want you to go through these & hand your reports to me each evening." It was not a pleasant task lying on my back as the underside of the lorries were caked in dried mud which had to be scraped off & with a breeze blowing the resulting dust landed on my face, hands & body. My inspections did find several lorries with cracked differential cases; these I marked with a centre punch to prevent the cracks spreading. [*an old trick still used today*] I had been on the task for some time when the Officer told me that he wanted 30 inspections per day; I told him that the six I completed daily were thoroughly done, any more and the inspections would be skimped, to that he did not reply and, I carried on until the rains came making outdoor inspection impossible.

I returned to the covered workshop and took it upon myself to work on a lorry that had just come in as all the other men were busy. I could do the work & there was a war on. The lorry was a 'Thornycroft' No. 22538, 34 Battery. The first task was to dismantle the engine & tighten number one big end which had worked loose, regrind the valves, clean the piston rings, clean the magneto & carburettor & fit new ignition leads. This was followed by a 'Locomobile' No. 27773 of 101 Battery, plus, a 'Commer' No. 30557 of 135 Battery both of which received similar attention.

I had been on this self-appointed task and working alone on overtime before the Workshop Officer noticed & enquired as to who had set me on this work. I simply said myself, I could not work in the downpour outside so am doing something useful as there is a war on. After a week of heavy rain, he came to 'ask' me if I would go out to bring a lorry in. One of our lorries loaded with shells had got into difficulties and come to a standstill in the middle of a road. The shells were transferred to another lorry and 2 or 3 fitters and a sergeant were sent out to the breakdown. They came back & said it was differential trouble which required a crane to bring it back, which we did not possess.

However, a lorry was going out in the general direction of the casualty and if all else failed, would pick me up later. So, I loaded up with timbers of various sizes and a kit of tools. We duly arrived at the site & following unloading I was left my own. I got to work by

removing the bolts holding the body to the chassis and, by levering
up and inserting timber packing an inch or two at a time, succeeded
in raising the body enough to allow me safe access to the differential.
The driving bevel gear was found to be damaged; this I removed &
took with me back to the workshop. Fortunately, we had a spare in
the stores, so next morning I set out again with the new bevel and
tins of oil and grease. The new part was fitted, the body secured, and
the lorry given a short test run in forward & reverse. This whole task
I accomplished single handed and, my aptitude for tackling awkward
jobs must have been noted as it was the forerunner of many to follow.
I was never ordered out to these jobs; the workshop officer had his
own method of approach to these matters. Late one night a signals
messenger arrived about 02.40 am to inform us that one of our lorries
loaded with shells and part of a column, had got into trouble in a
cutting & was blocking the track. The location was to be found by
turning left at Montauban church [*the track is still there today*]. Our
officer, in his usual way asked, "would you mind going out to a hold
up job, you know what we have in, if I send some of the fitters they
will not be seen again for about 4 days, you can have the box car and
take some tools & start away at once."

*Site of the breakdown, middle distance behind tree line, in the lane at
Montauban.*

I arrived at the site at about 3am & found our lorry at the bottom of the cutting skewed across the narrow lane with its driver's side front wheel in the drain ditch. The wheel hub was submerged in the mixtures of mud & water. The cutting had been lined with tree logs to prevent wear to the surface, the heavy rains had washed mud downhill & made the surface very slippery. At this place the banks of the cutting were high above, & on top were crowds of people shouting & swearing. It was sheeting down with rain & I flashed my torch upwards for a second through the mist, at the crowd above. I could just discern two or three officers wearing red cap bands, whether they were artillery staff officers I could not tell; certainly, a hubub was going on above me. One shouted down "Can't somebody do something, the poor ****** Infantry are getting it & the guns are being starved."

Having wrapped my legs in canvas as I had no gumboots, I stood in the ditch and worked by feel like a diver to trace the trouble. It soon became apparent that part of the steering gear was bent and to add to the problem, tree roots were tangled up in the mechanism. Eventually I was able by feel alone to trace the spilt pin and nut that held the assembly together and removed them. I then arranged a tow by connecting together all the other lorries stuck behind the casualty and, with a blast from my whistle the convoy began to move slowly back up the cutting to drier ground. As soon as a passage was clear a column of infantry threaded by, accompanied by pack mules carrying ammunition; all was silent as men & mules plodded downwards then on towards the front lines and the fighting. I heard later that a powerful towing tractor which ran on tracks & provided with heavy towing cables was stationed there in case of further trouble. The cutting was in use as a supply route to gun batteries near Contalmaison, Bazentin-le-Petit and Longueval.

I returned to our basin hollow as daylight was breaking & had a good wash & changed my wet through boots & muddy stained clothing & was given a hot mess tin of tea which was very welcome. This was the worst night time job I went to, on the Workshop Officer's, 'would you mind' principle. Later, one of my further journeys took me to Flers, near which place I saw some vehicle track marks I could not identify, which were later stated to have been tank track marks.

After promotion to N.C.O. I was posted to an Artillery Support Group and I had many opportunities of passing through & along many tracks, inclines & valleys. In many of the valleys the water had accumulated up to the lorry's hub cap level & was usually covered with slime. We very soon knew when the evil smelling water was disturbed, where many bodies had been interred at no great depth. While I mention this, I had been on a repair job & was returning to our basin hollow as passenger in a lorry just as dusk was falling, when the driver spotted some drier level ground that would allow us to miss some flooded ruts. As soon as we turned on to the 'dry spot' it did not take us long to realise that it was a place where dead bodies had been interred a few inches below ground. As the lorry wheels sank in they churned up a number of bodies, which produced a never to be forgotten vile stench; we quickly turned back on to the muddy, rutted road.

One day I had a sponge down with petrol, wise or unwise, I even poured it on my head. I had found that I had lice which I got from our lavatory pole, which some infantry had used as they passed by. I stripped & told the others not to come near me as I poured petrol on my head & wiped my body as it ran down, in the hope that it would disperse the lice; it did so & I was never troubled again with them.'

Also recalled was a supply run to deliver shells to a 9.2-inch howitzer.

'Offloading was achieved by rolling the shells off the lorry's tailboard on to large straw bags; the shells were not fitted with fuses so there was a good chance [*tongue in cheek*] that they would not explode. The sergeant of the gun's crew came over to chat and subsequently asked our man if he would like to fire the next round? Jumping at the chance

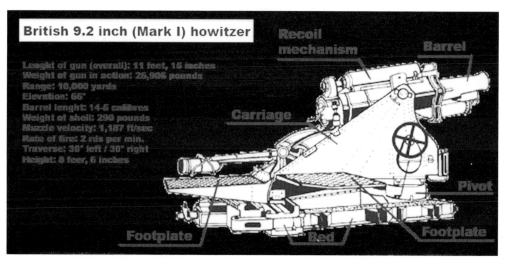

9.2-inch howitzer.

to send a 290lb 'greeting' up to 10,000 yards into enemy territory, he took the firing lanyard in his hands and prepared to give it a good pull on the command, Fire! It was not to be, an officer appeared in a fine old lather, 'get back to your lorry, you have no business here', then it became the sergeant's turn for a verbal battering.'

Who our informant was we shall probably never know. We can, however, confirm that he was recommended for promotion by P.D. Hamilton, Brigadier General Commanding H.A. (Heavy Artillery) XV Corps in October 1916.

Rank though could make a difference. In 1918 King George V observed the firing of the mighty 14-inch railway mounted gun 'Boche Buster'; the shell caused immense damage to an important railway installation used by the enemy at Douai in Belgium. The king though was within his rights, as the nominal head of all British Armed Services he was entitled to check whether this expensive piece of equipment worked – each shell cost £4,435 at today's values. Royalty had a long-standing interest in artillery, the 'Sun King' Louis XIV of France ordered the words *Ultima Ratio Regum* (The Final Argument of Kings) to be cast into the barrels of his guns. King George V outranked our fitter and Boche Buster was the means of sending his 'Final Argument' to his cousin the kaiser.

Railway gun, 'Boche Buster'. King George V (5th from left) observes the firing.

Ever more artillery ammunition was consumed by the BEF during the Somme fighting. Between 26 June and 9 July, 526,000 rounds were fired weighing 75,000 tons and all of this dangerous and heavy freight was moved by the unsung heroes of the ASC.

The BEF Enters the Tyre Business

The tyre is a critical component of any wheeled vehicle; in the case of MT, it is the final link between the engine and the road surface where the power developed is transformed into rotative movement. The vital, yet simple steel strip acting as a tyre, fitted to a wooden wheel, prevents the wheel from disintegrating in a very short time. The down side of such 'tyres' was the high noise levels produced on cobbled streets and the tyre's ability to dig ruts into road surfaces that were not macadamised, which included most of the roads beyond city boundaries in Great Britain and Europe. Tyres fitted to motor vehicles were mostly of the solid rubber type. The idea that pneumatic tyres could be fitted to commercial vehicles was regarded in 1914 as 'fanciful' by some of the foremost experts (both civil and military) in the field of MT at that time. Private car and motor cycle owners began to use pneumatic tyres from an early period, but the pneumatics suffered from one great disadvantage not of their own making – a constant plague of punctures caused by the many hundreds of thousands of horse shoe nails and flints that lay in wait for any passing driver.

Owners were faced with a stark choice, a much softer ride free of constant jolting and far less wear and tear to the vehicle and the roads, but stopping for multiple puncture repairs and/or expensive tyre replacement. Products were marketed with the claim to eliminate the problems of punctures. Included in these products was a system of multi-inner tubes, operating on the principle that at least one of the tubes would survive the multiple flat tyres that often occurred. This system was very expensive to produce and to purchase and, as with a good many 'quick fix' ideas, it quickly withered on the vine. Filling the tyre with a semi-solid substance, similar to that used today by car manufacturers who do not supply a spare wheel, was an option but quality control in the production of the filling varied greatly as did the results. In hot weather, vehicles were found with flat areas where the wheel was in contact with the road. Perhaps that's where the old, unhelpful, saying

Advertisement in very poor taste for Clincher tyres.

'it's only flat at the bottom' originates? Seeing the scale of the puncture problem, the BEF designed and constructed a 'Nail Collector' which cruised the roads picking up horse shoe nails, shell splinters and other ferrous detritus. It is believed that a similar machine came into use on UK roads.

Solid tyres are just that, solid pieces of rubber formed into a circular form to fit over a wheel. Punctures cannot happen to solid tyres but unfortunately, they have two major deficiencies. Firstly, they cannot dissipate the heat generated by friction between the tyre and the road surface, and if not allowed to cool down, the tyre will start to disintegrate and the vehicle will be out of service. Any prolonged running at speeds above 10 mph will generate destructive heat. On heavy vehicles, it was found that 10 mph extended the life of the tyres by reducing the heat generated. The BEF imposed the 10 mph limit on its lorries for this reason, plus fuel economy and road safety.

Secondly, the solid tyre was 'bald', a heinous offence today but the reason for the absence of a tread pattern was entirely practical; tread patterns cause friction and generate heat, so even a relatively short run would have induced expensive tyre disintegration. The area of contact between the solid tyre and the road surface was equal to an average of 20 square inches. If the vehicle had an all-up weight of 6 tons, each square inch of tyre supported 224lbs. The pneumatic tyre with its lower ground pressure greatly reduced road wear and improved safety. The combination of bald/smooth tyre and loose, wet or slippery road surfaces caused a constant risk of skidding and led to extended braking distances being imposed. To minimise the risk of collision, BEF lorry drivers were instructed to leave a gap of 75ft from the vehicle in front. Even with relatively low speeds, tyre wear on the Western Front was colossal with an average life of 4,000 miles reducing to 2,000 miles depending on location and loads carried.

As demand for tyres greatly exceeded pre-war production facilities, rapid, new factory building took place. The Dunlop Company based in inner Birmingham is a good example. Located in the already crowded Aston area of the city, no further expansion was possible, leading the company to build a new factory on a greenfield site near Erdington. As most of the workers lived in Aston and there was not as yet a road connecting the new factory to its workers' dwellings, the company resorted to using narrow boats on the Tame Valley Canal to transport people to and from work. How the new factory acquired the name 'Fort Dunlop' is still a mystery, although it was also known as 'The Stronghold of the British Tyre Industry' which may have had some bearing on the case. Around 1,000 of Dunlop's employees were quickly called up for service in 1914; the company made it known that they would pay half wages to the men's dependants and that their jobs would be kept open for them.

The supply of solid tyres from British manufacturers grew to 11,500 per week, with a further 13,500 from America to serve the needs of the many American vehicles in use by the BEF. February 1917 saw the visit to France of a deputation of the 'Solid Tyre Committee of the Society of Motor Manufactures and Traders' to enquire into the storage and use of tyres by the BEF. A problem had developed, a small percentage of solid tyres 'bursting' when being pressed onto the wheels. The committee quickly realised that this was a quality issue and took immediate steps to rectify the situation. Mention was also made of the high tyre wear being experienced on the Western Front; the pavé roads proved to be efficient tyre destroyers. Recovering vehicles that had skidded off the road was causing tyres to come off the wheel completely when sideways pulling was required to regain the road.

Sunlight was discovered to be the enemy of tyres; darkened warehouses were constructed to keep the tyres in good condition prior to issue. Marcosson reported in *The Business of War* being shown a warehouse that contained 44,000 pneumatic tyres, 40,000 inner tubes and 17,000 solid tyres. Drivers were supplied with a map showing the location of tyre presses and, in the event of tyre damage, the vehicle was taken directly to the press where his spare tyre would be pressed onto the wheel. Should the driver not have a spare tyre, one would be provided; bureaucracy being the oxygen of government, the driver's unit would then be invoiced for the cost. It was really a case of 'this is the best we can get, we have to make it work'.

The solid tyre has never gone away, they are still in use on fork-lift trucks, fairground rides and children's scooters to name but a few. As for 'bald' tyres, it has been noticed that racing cars are so equipped.

Petrol the Life Blood of MT

Petrol: from the Greek, Petra (rock) and Oleum (oil). That used by the BEF had first to be imported into Great Britain as crude oil before being processed into petrol, decanted into tins, transported by sea to France and distributed to MT depots before finally reaching the fuel tank of a lorry. The 3-ton payload lorry consumed a gallon of petrol per 5 miles. This means of supplying petrol was expensive and consumed valuable shipping space. An early attempt at economising petrol consumption came about in May 1915 when drivers were to be asked to switch off their engines when not on the move. S.S. 400 went further, on page 3, item 7, *'**Running Engines:** An engine is not to be kept running when the vehicle is stationary.'*

All petrol was distributed in 2-gallon tins for smaller vehicles and 4-gallon tins for lorries. By mid-1916, Fourth Army alone was consuming 12,000 gallons per day or, 6,000 empty tins to be taken to a bulk refilling point every day. Small bulk tankers were trialled, however, it was quickly discovered that refuelling a column of lorries took far too long; over five hours being required to fill 110 lorries. Replenishment of the divisional cars, ambulances, vans and mobile workshops was also achieved by using the petrol tin which was quicker and far more flexible, especially in providing petrol to remote locations in a hurry.

The manufacture of petrol tins was eventually moved to France. In an amazing feat of organisation, an entire factory was operating in France just nine days after commencing the move. Tankers also began to deliver refined petrol direct to France. Filled tins were moved by rail; each railway van held 1,200 gallons of petrol and forty vans made up a train, four trains left each day. As the amount of petrol consumed rose ever higher, an Inspector of Petrol Consumption was appointed to report to the War Office.

The war had become like no other that had preceded it; a commentator declared that it was an engineer's war and the first to be propelled by petrol. With many thousands of motor vehicles now supplying the army's needs, the massive military operations that were taking place were ultimately reliant on the uninterrupted supply of petrol. The lorry offered mobility with one hand but in return demanded liquid gold, the price of which cost lives to deliver.

By 1918, if the private vehicle owner could find any petrol for sale, the cost was 3s 11½d per gallon, equivalent to £9.08p in 2018.

The Magneto: No Spark, No explosion, No power

The magneto was a device that was bolted onto the vehicle's engine in order to provide the current that produced the spark which then exploded the petrol and air mixture, the force of the explosion forcing the pistons downward providing the power to turn the wheels. Prior to the outbreak of war, Great Britain was almost entirely dependent on the German firm of Bosch for the supply of magnetos, 90 per cent of the yearly supply of magnetos for use in the UK came from their Stuttgart factory. British firms mainly took the view that it was not worth their while to invest in the expertise and machinery to produce magnetos for the home market as Bosch were in such a powerful position and could easily undercut the price to a point that British firms could not compete.

But on 4 August 1914 all that changed – the supply of magnetos quickly dried up. America was able to supply a certain number, but an assured supply of the correct specification was urgently needed. Mass production of magnetos was by no means easy to organise. The hand of bureaucracy was never far away and quickly showed itself as early as August 1914, warning would-be manufacturers that even in the dire emergency the country found itself in; any infringement of the Bosch patent *'will lead to trouble'*. Drawings had to be produced for production engineers to interpret before materials to the exact specification were ordered and machines set up to begin production, together with all the necessary gauges to ensure quality and the training of tool setters and machine operators.

Fortunately for Great Britain, the firm of British Thomson-Houston had, been working on magneto development at its Coventry factory for twelve months before war broke out and also, the firm of Thompson & Bennett of Birmingham who, unusually for a British company and through huge investment, were producing the modest amount of twenty-five magnetos per week. The partners recalled *'it was a heart-breaking business and time after time we faced the position whether it was worthwhile going on'*. Great Britain also found herself embarrassingly short of optical glass, despite repeated warnings from the glass makers Chance Brothers that the country was entirely dependent on Germany for optical glass in the use of gun sights, binoculars and microscopes.

After overcoming myriad difficulties in a short time Mr Peter Bennett recalled in *The Great Munition Feat*:

Last of all, we had the difficulty which everybody has experienced, and which was particularly acute in a new industry – the shortage of proper machinery, and the training of butchers, bakers and candlestick makers to the work of making the magnetos.

Advertisement for Hall magneto.

A list of some of the materials required to produce a magneto include: varnished silk, cambric, paper, ruby mica, tinfoil, aluminium and copper die castings, Egyptian cotton tape, silk tubes of fine bore, ball bearings, carbon brushes, ebonite rod and sheet. The silk was produced in Japan and reached the UK via America.

'Magnetos in Service', an article in the trade press dated 1916 describes the American made HECO magneto as promising power and reliability. Reproduced below is a letter describing the experience of actually using the machine in question.

D.D.S&T. Fourth Army (Deputy Director of Supplies & Transport)

HECO Magnetos
1. *Considerable trouble has been experienced with this make of Magneto by this Corps.*
2. *The chief faults reported are:*
    (a) *Collecting ring drive being taken by the lead wire causing the wire to shear and the driving ring to come apart.*
    (b) *The distributor driving wheel works loose. The driving shaft becomes loose on the armature.*
    (c) *The primary winding becomes disconnected from the core on earth end.*
    (d) *The make and break spring either breaks or breaks its stud.*
3. *Spare parts are very difficult to obtain.*
4. *As the design is evidently very faulty, may the issue of these magnetos be discontinued and those at present giving trouble be exchanged for others of a proved make, please.*

(signed) J. Hamilton, Major
For S.M.T.O. Australian Corps (Senior Mechanical Transport Officer)
18/9/18

The above quite alarming situation could be the result of expanding production too quickly before proper training has been carried out. The present writer witnessed several such production failures while working in British industry.

Sparking Plugs

To this day, all petrol driven machines need sparking plugs, the last link in the electrical system that explodes the fuel mixture. S.S. 364, issued Christmas Day 1917, expressed concern that the demand for sparking plugs had become very heavy. Officers in charge of MT were to take great care to see that plugs were not changed if all they required was cleaning and adjustment. Unlike modern plugs, those used a hundred years ago could be repaired but, human nature being what it is, 'one in three' of the plugs sent to the UK for repair were missing the terminal nut without which the plug was useless. Terminal nuts could easily be dropped by frozen fingers working in darkness, a few spare nuts being seen by drivers as an essential item in the tool box. Checks were called for on the storage of spare plugs carried on vehicles to ensure that they would not be damaged. The humble terminal nut had become the horse shoe nail – small, inexpensive and without which the army transport would be brought to a halt.

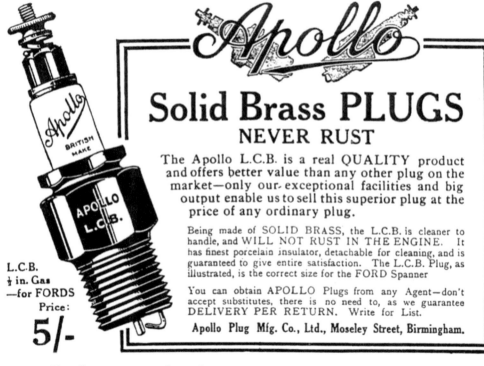

The all-important sparking plug.

Chapter 9

Running the Loops (Supply)

Parks, Columns and Trains: the terms are often confusing as Parks did not stay still and Trains did not run on tracks. Parks utilised MT and carried gun ammunition from the Heads of Steel as far forward as road conditions allowed. Columns also used MT and carried stores between the railheads and the divisional re-filling points. Trains used HT and provided the final link from the re-filling points into the forward areas.

A Supply Column consisted of:

45	3-ton lorries
16	30cwt lorries
2	cars
7	motor cycles
4	lorries used as workshops and stores
337	Other Ranks
5	officers

A Train consisted of:

378	horses
125	waggons
17	carts
30	push bikes
402	Other Ranks
26	Officers

Supply Dump, near Albert, in the ferocious winter of 1916/17.

Long portrayed, often quite unjustly, as being bereft of foresight and imagination, the army staff were proved correct when they decided before the outbreak of war that re-supply must not rely solely upon MT. There was not a powered, wheeled vehicle in existence at that time that could traverse broken-up terrain while carrying a full load. Given the actual ground conditions that developed on the Western Front, consisting of shell holes, trenches, mud fields and extensive flooding, there still isn't. On the other hand, a horse can go almost anywhere a man can go. As the war continued, the role of MT developed as pre-war trials had shown that MT made a reliable link between the railheads and the refilling points where HT took over responsibility for onward carriage. This major task became known as 'running the loops' an endless loop of supply, most likely out and back by different routes to ease road congestion and alleviate the endless problem of damage to the roads. On 11 October 1916, the Quartermaster General's Department issued a warning to army commanders: *'To see that their roads are maintained, and that excessive traffic is not run over such roads when repairs are necessary.' (see National Archive, WO 95/32)*

The year 1917 dawned, the Battle of the Somme had fizzled out in the sleet and mists of November 1916. The enemy had retreated to his previously prepared position known to the BEF as the Hindenburg Line which had been partly constructed by the use of forced civilian labour. February witnessed the BEF gradually moving forward unable to quite believe that the enemy trenches were now unoccupied. Murderous clashes did take place, in particular at a natural feature known to the BEF as 'Boom Ravine' located a kilometre east of the village of Grandcourt and shown on the French I.G.N map 2407 *est* as the 'Grande Royarts'.

Life for the ASC revolved around two distinct roles: supplying the 'quiet' sectors where coal, mail, comforts, food and concert parties were the main categories carried, and active sectors, in particular when a 'show' was planned or in progress. On the active sectors, ammunition, food, reinforcements and evacuation of the wounded were the priorities. The supply of water caused immediate problems as the retreating enemy had poisoned all known wells. GHQ sent in a request to the War Office for several auxiliary petrol companies to be sent to France in the role of water carriers. As is the way of governments, these much-needed vehicles were refused. It apparently mattered not one jot to the mandarins of Whitehall that their own soldiers, under the baleful glare of an extremely hostile enemy, were going short of water, the absolute essential of life itself.

The BEF, cast back on its own resources, had to cobble together anything that might just work. For the most part in 1917, the Western Front hardly moved at all and, in a reversal of the supply arrangements of previous campaigns, where mobile armies foraged (stole/paid) for food and static armies eventually starved, it was now the static army that was well fed and supplied with all its needs.

The columns were usually divided into two parts, one part loaded at the nearest railhead which then returned to the hard-standing area to carry out maintenance and inspections on the vehicles to ensure that all was well. Contrary to the beliefs of most of the BEF, the ASC did engage in military activities such as rifle drill and route marching to a very high standard. Meanwhile, the other part of the column would have proceeded where required to the refilling points to unload. The next day the tasks would be reversed. By these methods the wear on the roads and vehicles was kept down, maintenance improved and the men were kept fit for whatever trials the war might throw at them.

MT Driver Tom Bromley recalled:

We were under stress, if you can use that word. The question of rest didn't enter in to it; it was night and day, get what rest you could. But the ammunition had to be delivered where it was needed, regardless of the comfort of the individual. And I would say this, that our boys –practically all of whom were volunteers in the first instance – knew what was required of them and didn't hesitate to carry out the tasks assigned to them, with a cheerful heart. They were very efficient in doing the job, keeping the lorries on the road and making sure that the guns received the ammunition that they wanted. Now this wasn't done without danger of course. Sometimes under great difficulties, not only of shell fire and there was great confusion, breakdowns, horse transport in the way, troops trying to come up and down, ambulances coming back with wounded – oh, tremendous confusion, sometimes – but nevertheless, we got the job done, without complaint. Never any question of any hesitation in getting on with it.

Lorry convoy, artist's impression – Mike O'Brien.

As experience was gained, loading became a smart operation. As an example, twelve 'B' Type buses converted to lorries were loaded from railway vans with food and fodder for 2,000 men and 2,200 horses in one hour. The voluminous amount of mail was usually carried by one 3-ton lorry, another being assigned to carry petrol, oils, grease, paraffin and calcium carbide, which substance when mixed with water produced acetylene gas for use in vehicle headlamps. Frozen meat was also carried after it was cut up by expert butchers at the Head of Steel; these men were so skilful that scales were not needed beyond an occasional check, Tommy must not be short-changed. The same was true of cheese and butter, the 'grocers' working by eye without error when cutting up bulk supplies into the correct weight for rations.

The year of 1917 proved more than usually eventful for the BEF. The Battle of Arras opened on 9 April when Canadian infantry, supported by the Royal Artillery stormed the heights of Vimy Ridge, a triumph of organisation and planning. The attack could not be fully exploited due to the shell-torn nature of the landscape preventing re-supply. The Battle of Bullecourt, a combined tank and infantry attack launched on 11 April facing Bullecourt (8 miles north-east of Bapaume), failed with disastrous losses to the Australian and British troops engaged. The French army attack on the Chemin des Dames was repulsed so conclusively and with such great loss to the already sorely tried French troops that a serious mutiny ensued. For some time later, the French

Australian Troops, Bullecourt, 1917.

were not able to contemplate attacking the invader, instead they would defend their positions until time-consuming reforms had been completed.

This left the BEF alone to confront the German army with such unremitting violence that the invader was forced to oppose the BEF and could not contemplate an all-out attack on the weakened French. The Belgian city of Ypres beckoned. Situated at its nearest point, only 22 miles from the North Sea and surrounded by a ring of low hills that were occupied by the enemy, Ypres was not by any measure, an ideal position for the BEF to hold. As the last relatively small area of Belgium not overrun by Germany and defended for three years at great cost in life by the BEF, Ypres was also vital to the defence of the Channel Ports. Only one and a half days' march from Ypres would find the enemy in possession of the entire Belgian coast and the opportunity to seriously disrupt the shipping lifelines that fed the Western Front. These were the stark political and military realities facing the Allies in 1917. Let us make no mistake, all could very easily be lost.

In days when the world was at peace, Ypres could use canals, roads and railways to export her famous towelling cloth to the world, 'diaper'

Daimler and German prisoners pass through Ypres.

being a corruption of Cloth of Ypres. The riches produced by the cloth trade built the famous Cloth Hall, cathedral and the town fortifications.

The ruination of the great city began in October 1914 when the BEF fought what became known as the First Battle of Ypres. The relentless destruction of the city would go on for the next three years. An ASC officer, A.M. Beatson, seeing the ruins of Ypres for the first time in 1915, was stricken by a sense of utter loneliness such as he had never experienced; he became convinced that Ypres would be haunted by the ghosts of the thousands of soldiers who had already died in the defence of the city.

He commented on the efforts of his men to communicate with the local people and how easily '*deux biers see-voo-play madam*' came to be adopted. The present writer, due to years of practice, can vouch that the linguistic skills of the Tommies of old still work today. The sale of spirits had been banned by GHQ but, in certain cafes, requesting a '*van blank Ecosse*' would produce a whisky and soda!

The map shows the Salient bulging outwards from Ypres for 6 miles and surrounded on three sides by the enemy. The Salient would shrink slightly then expand to encompass the heavily fortified village of Passchendaele. A massive mining attack was launched by the BEF on 7 June 1917 when nineteen enormous mines destroyed much of the German defensive positions on the Messines Ridge outside Ypres. Although devastating, the success could not be quickly followed up due to the difficulties of movement over the shattered ground, which also caused delays in the preparation of the 'jumping off' trenches needed to continue the assault.

The offensive was renewed on 31 July to become known as the Third Battle of Ypres or Passchendaele. 'General Rain' soon threw in his hand pouring millions of tons of water onto the already pulverised ground which had been subjected to an opening BEF bombardment of 4,250,000 shells. The delicate drainage system which kept the land fertile was utterly destroyed, converting the Salient into an extremely dangerous quagmire capable of swallowing man or horse without trace. It was into this dreadful morass that the ASC was to set out upon its most arduous task of the entire war. Men, horses, mules, ambulances, lorries and buses would all be engaged in the battle with the mud of the Salient. Running the loops was never so destroying of the will as was that of Ypres. In order to keep the traffic flowing, the men of 319 Road

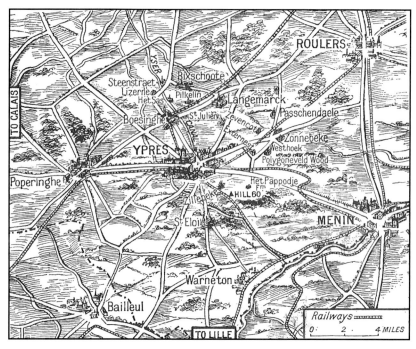

Map of Ypres Salient.

Construction Coy, Royal Engineers found themselves working deep in the endless mud-fields of the Salient. The following diary extracts give terse descriptions of the dangers the men faced in their daily tasks of keeping the roads open in October 1917:

> *Bricklayers repairing bridge on the Voormezelle – St. Eloi Rd. 4 men filling shell holes.*
> *Levelling the sides of Monmouth Road – work stopped from 10am to 1.45pm due to heavy shelling by the enemy.*
> *Relaying the Monmouth Sleeper Road (roads constructed from wooden sleepers to allow passage across the deep mud)*
> *Two 'Emergency Lorries' again deliver macadam for road repairs – hours of work are 07.30 to 4.30.*
> *A large shell hole at Hooge – 6 lorries sent with men and materials – road restored to traffic.*
> *27 lorry loads sent to Leinster Road – same day several men of another unit were killed or wounded by shell fire on*

the Menin Road, 5 of our men distinguished themselves by rushing to the aid of victims while themselves under the heavy shell fire.

The Menin Road leads south-east from Ypres and was the scene of some of the heaviest fighting during First and Third Ypres. The road is now guarded by the famous Menin Gate. The Menin Road itself, was immortalised by the paintings of John Nash who had served with the Artists Rifles. Even with the unrelenting thunder of the guns, small side shows still took place around Ypres as a diary records: 13 August, '*20 lorries on detachment for salvage work in the back area, Light railway run to dumps by U.S.A. Railway troops, trains arrived 30 minutes earlier than usual…Shortage of drivers with men on leave – 12th December thaw precautions; no lorries on the roads except post.*' The post was vital for the morale of the troops.

Second Army Traffic Orders of January 1917 strictly forbade overtaking by buses or lorries travelling in the same direction. The orders

YPRES. RUINS OF THE CLOTH HALL, SEEN FROM ST. MARTIN'S CATHEDRAL. FRAGMENTS OF THE LATTER ARE VISIBLE IN THE FOREGROUND

Ruins of the famous Cloth Hall, Ypres which was fully restored post war.

also contained notes on the management of horses. Divisions were charged with the responsibility of constructing *'special tracks so as to ensure that roads are avoided as far as possible by watering parties. Whenever horses going to water have to cross a traffic road, an Officer will accompany them to ensure that traffic is not delayed.'*

A note in an MT unit war diary recorded: *'Prisoner, Pte. Lewis to Rouen for two years hard labour.'* For such a punishment, the offence must have been very grave, as elsewhere in this work Field Punishment No.1 was awarded for being drunk while on duty. Long prison sentences were not usually handed down, as it could encourage malingerers to avoid their duty and live out the war in safety while others were being killed or wounded in their place.

As the year 1917 drew to a close the BEF found itself in a position it had never before experienced – the supply of gun ammunition exceeded the ability of the gunners to fire it. The gun barrels began to wear out faster than they could be replaced. Prolonged and intensive firing left behind traces of picric acid in the barrels which, together with the

A very stark reminder of the real dangers faced by lorry drivers.

friction of the shell being forced out at immense speed, caused barrel wear. If this condition was allowed to go unchecked the gun would become dangerous and inaccurate. In a mild case of irony, the plenty enjoyed by the gunners was the result of Geddes' transport reforms. The seeds were now planted that grew into the 'umbrella' that would shield the infantry in the Battles of the Hundred Days that came to fruition in the summer of 1918.

Chapter 10

1918 The Year of Decision

This proved to be a momentous year for the BEF and the Allies. The previous year had been marked by a succession of trials – Vimy Ridge had fallen but the Battles of Arras and Bullecourt had led, to say the least, disappointing outcomes. The French Army, so sorely tried by a succession of disastrous offensives, finally cracked leading to a widespread mutiny, following which, the troops would defend but not attack. The Third Battle of Ypres was so vicious and protracted that it still echoes to this day in the soul of nations. The mass artillery, tank and infantry assault at Cambrai was initially a spectacular success but was undone mainly due to lack of fresh troops in reserve to exploit the breach made in the enemy's lines. The church bells had been rung throughout the UK to celebrate the 'victory' at Cambrai, but all too soon the enemy counter-attacked and the hard-won gains were lost.

The prospects for the Allies in 1918 looked bleak; the BEF was tasked to take over more sectors of the front from the French who were busily engaged in restoring morale and a belief in victory among their long-suffering infantry. Allied intelligence began to hear whispers of a forthcoming enemy offensive. Germany was running out of food, time and resources. The enemy's civilian population had endured the 'Turnip Winter', that great staple of the German meal, the potato, had all but disappeared from the shops. At sea, the Allied navies had sealed off Germany's supplies of imports. Seen through the eyes of the enemy's high command, the solution to Germany's problems would be an enormous last throw of the dice. The over-extended and under manned BEF would be crushed and chased into the sea; French morale would collapse and the recently arrived and untried Americans would receive a shattering blow from which they could not recover. These assumptions proved utterly wrong; numerous ferocious and costly attacks were made upon the Allies, but defeat of the Anglo/French/American armies would never happen.

A narrow-gauge battlefield railway, artist's impression – Mike O'Brien.

For the Germans, the seeds of destruction had begun to germinate and their weak transport and supply system would make a great contribution to their downfall. Due to lack of rubber, the enemy's lorries ran mostly on steel rims which degraded the roads at an alarming rate. Petrol was also in short supply preventing the fast, forward movement of food and ammunition. The available horse power was also in serious decline. The horses were expected to work harder on half of their daily ration, at the same time veterinary care declined as did the day to day care the horses should have received, due to the inexperience of troops assigned to HT who had no real knowledge of the horses' needs. For example, the German Army's own records revealed that between July 1917 and May 1918, 83,384 horses had died from malnutrition and overwork. Had the German High Command bothered to study and absorb the words of Sun Tzu, they would have 'discovered' that: *'If fodder and grain are provided at the right times the horses will draw the chariots easily. If there is an abundance of axle grease the chariots can easily carry the men.'*

To embark upon offensives that would cost hundreds of thousands of lives without the vital transport arrangements can only be described as the height of criminal stupidity.

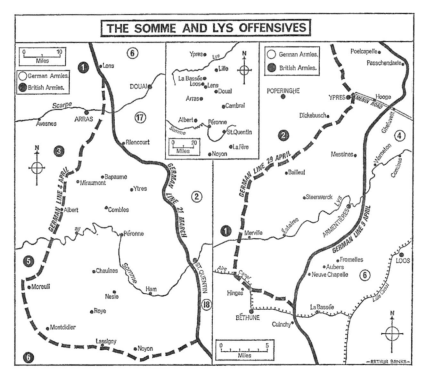

Map of the German Spring Offensive 1918.

For the ASC the year 1918 began quietly enough running the loops with mail, food and ammunition, the setting up of depots in the newly extended front and feeding in supplies of everything deemed of necessity by the BEF. Third Army began to prepare very strong in-depth defences backed up by advance dumps of supplies established by the ASC. Fifth Army, which had over extended itself to cover the former French position, was in a totally different situation. Short of manpower and with a home government that was by now nervous of sending out more troops to reinforce the BEF, Fifth Army simply did not have enough men to man the front lines and build the vitally-needed numbers of in-depth positions that would blunt and then disrupt the enemy. When the predicted blow fell on 21 March, Fifth Army began to crumble and panic ensued in London.

In reality, the enemy succeeded in putting his head 'into a bag' where he could be assailed from three sides. Ultimately, he lost his best soldiers – the *Stoßtruppen* (shock troops) who could not be replaced in vast numbers. These men had, in a country suffering acute food shortages, been better fed than their comrades; it was all for nothing in the end.

As did all efficient armies, the BEF had well-developed contingency plans to be activated in the case of an enemy breakthrough. Crucial to the success of the plan was traffic control. The ASC Journal for March-April 1918 published an article during the time of the German Offensive, explaining in detail the BEF's traffic arrangements as they greatly affected how the ASC did its vital work. The following is an abridged version of the article:

When the actual fighting men begin to fall back danger arises of the men behind them being turned into a disorganised mob. Good generalship can prevent this. It is commonly supposed that the ASC and other auxiliary services have a 'cushy' time. Never was there a greater misconception. During our Army's retirement in France, the enemy sought to isolate the troops in front of him by cutting off all communications to the rear. Roads for miles back were hammered by heavy artillery. Cross-roads and junctions bombarded as were any roads close to railheads.

But 'touch' must be maintained. Consequently, ASC drivers whether of horse or motor-lorries have to make their way through the hail of projectiles. After winning through they must return and risk it all again. All munitions are moved in this manner. As the front line falls back the transport has to reorganise itself in an orderly fashion ignoring the shells that may be dropping close by.

In all circumstances traffic is directed as it is in London. Frequently there are ex-London policemen controlling it. The forward and rearward streams are kept strictly apart as any departure from this rule would result in a general rout.

Guns and ambulances go up and down in the same manner. The 'Traffic Control' stands at every street corner, at every cross-road, and whatever switch-road has been opened. What he says counts as law, for he is Lord of the highways and all must obey him. No cheerful task his, either. No matter how hot may be the corner he occupies, he has to 'stick it'

ASC scrapyard, Northern France.

so long as he remains uninjured. Immediately he gets 'pipped' another autocrat steps into his place.

All main roads are well known to the enemy, who is able to fire on them 'by the map'. In other words, he knows just how to lay his guns to make a particular section of road practically impassable. Road-making forms a far more important part of the operations than is generally realised, whether troops are advancing or retiring. Particularly in the latter case unduly congested traffic may be the precursor of disaster; therefore, every general tries his utmost to avoid it. Conditions may easily arise in which the heavy motor-lorries now used in such numbers by both sides become something of an embarrassment. They cannot be driven over ploughed fields or any kind of rough country, as can light horsed vehicles. Made roads are needed to carry MT and in a withdrawal this class of traffic demands careful handling if dangerous 'blocks' are to be prevented. These problems are not left to chance but are carefully thought beforehand since a competently handled army has its plans laid for a move in either direction at any time.

An advancing army always forms big supply 'dumps' (or depots) of various kinds of war material close behind its line of advance. Buildings of different sorts spring up to meet the hundred and one requirements of the troops, and nowadays also there are the field railways. Shifting back this impedimenta is seldom possible. Consequently, it is destroyed to prevent it from falling into the enemy's hands. Sometimes he may advance so rapidly that this cannot be done. But generally, the kerosene tin or the dynamite has done its work before the enemy reaches depots of abandoned stores, buildings or railways that would be of use to him.

Looking at a broader picture than the above account, it has to be said that Fifth Army's traffic control arrangements left a lot to be desired. When the German blow fell on 21 March, 6,784 German guns opened fire on a 40-mile front of Third and Fifth Armies, a four-and-a-half hour bombardment followed by mixed high-explosive, mustard gas and lachrymatory (tear gas) shells. When the shelling ceased, 3,500 mortars opened fire on the dazed defenders before the storm troopers arrived in the banks of fog. The BEF's movements became disrupted as civilian traffic poured onto the roads mixed with retreating soldiers, all hampering attempts to re-supply those troops still holding out and very possibly cut off.

With the enemy hot on their heels, some troops detailed to destroy stores opted for self-preservation instead. Some good came of this as the Germans fell upon the goods and began to plunder them on a grand scale. Their own government propaganda led them to believe that the BEF was starving and badly clothed. What they actually came across were bountiful supplies of the food that they had not seen for years, accompanied by the discovery of rum supplies in plenty leading to

Albion lorry with troops going up the line. (Courtesy of R. Pullen)

large, impromptu, alfresco feasts and a mindset that said, 'the war can wait'. Brand-new clothing was also included in the booty, resulting in German soldiers kitting themselves out with new underclothes and socks. The greatest prize was the 'British Warm' the double-sided waistcoat made from goatskins; smelly, but just the thing for a freezing night spent in the open air. Some good for the Allies came of these feasts; in several places the enemy's advance was slowed and some cohesion lost, plus German soldiers began to realise that they had been lied to – the BEF was not a starving ill-equipped rabble. It's true that some units did surrender rapidly but this was mainly due to a sense of isolation that came about with the initial German thrust that had taken place in thick fog. Men found themselves surrounded and cut off from their comrades, a dire situation when morale quickly collapses.

With both rail and road services out of action, ration supply was interrupted for a short time but thanks to a decision taken by local commanders, troops were told to help themselves to anything that they could eat or carry from dumps that were in imminent danger of being overrun by the enemy. Was whisky left behind? One of the abiding mysteries/tales of the BEF relates to whisky. The amber liquid did not reach the rank and file whose staple was rum, but there are many accounts of whisky being freely and abundantly available in front line officers' dug-outs. Charles Lander (see *Lander's War*) tells of three officers who, he suspected, were fired up by whisky and decided to explore no man's land; all three were either captured or killed. As the sale of spirits was prohibited anywhere near the battle fronts, it must be concluded that large stocks of Scotch were moved forward by clandestine methods. Did the ASC play a part in this subterfuge? We shall never know.

On 11 April, 256 MT Coy found itself caught up in the German Offensive on the River Lys:

> *British infantry had crossed the bridge, it was then blown up & stores destroyed. Unit carrying, pickets, barbed wire, hurdles and other necessary material to GHQ Defence Lines. Then proceeded to Auchy Au Bois to build a hard standing using shale and slag to accommodate 74 lorries.*

In Fifth Army area, and caught up in the hurricane of modern battle, Private, R. Dunn, M/39663, 18th Special Coy ASC, died of wounds received due to enemy shell fire on 20 April 1918, aged 32. He was the brother of J. Dunn of 32, Hawthorn Street, Glasgow. Nowhere was safe.

With the opening of the German attacks in March, a war of movement had developed. Although this at last raised the possibility of out-manoeuvring the enemy, it also meant that the 'great slayer' artillery, had become semi-mobile again. Guns quickly changed firing positions before they could be located and subjected to counter-battery fire and shells often came from three directions at once. The enemy had been able to establish himself just 10 miles from the great transportation hub of Amiens; many of Third and Fifth army's Heads of Steel had been lost, including much of the narrow-gauge systems.

Included in the transport losses were the barges and steam tugs of the Inland Waterways Companies who, to deny their use to the enemy, had scuttled their craft and destroyed lock gates before they left. Many of the light railway staff were evacuated by lorries that had been allotted to road repair companies as the trainloads of road stone required were locked into the disrupted railways – all hope of keeping the roads in

Narrow-gauge railway destroyed by shell-fire.

repair had gone. All concerned headed in a westerly direction as fast as the traffic conditions would allow. The number of lorries lost stood at 380, a small fraction of the total serving with the BEF, but due to production constraints more difficult to replace than an artillery piece. Also lost were a number of artillery tractors used for the haulage of heavy guns. In the seeming chaos of March and April, the BEF fired off a figure approaching 9,000,000 of 18-pounder shells out of around 15,000,000 fired. Even this prodigious expenditure did not exhaust ammunition stocks as more kept pouring into the French Channel ports. It was in fact a war of *matériel* that Germany could not win.

Countess Haig writing in her biography of her husband, Sir Douglas Haig in 1936, explained the cause of the BEF's problems as follows:

> *Douglas pointed out that what was wrong was not Gough's generalship but the fact that the War Cabinet had so weakened the forces and failed to make adequate arrangements for keeping the divisions up to strength that there were not enough men to withstand the German assault. He drew attention to the fact that so many troops had been withdrawn from France that at the beginning of the battle there were about 100,000 fewer men available than in the previous year, and that this depleted force had been attacked by a force three times larger than what they had to face in the previous year. To these difficulties had to be added the fact that the Government had ordered the British to take over more of the French line, so that the depleted numbers of troops were holding fully one-fifth more than they had in the previous autumn. In spite of Douglas's explanations, the War Cabinet decided that the Commander of the 5th Army was at fault and he was therefore brought home.*

Many would argue that the countess was a biased historian but, keep in mind much of written history is just that. The countess and her son had to endure decades of downright hatred directed at Haig's memory, in particular following his early death.

May 1918 brought severe railway problems for the BEF. One of the most important lateral rail lines, that of Hazebrouck–Amiens–St Just, had to be abandoned to the enemy bringing the railway system into a state of near paralysis.

Thornycroft lorry, artist's impression – Mike O'Brien.

This was a crisis in the fullest sense of the word; without supplies reaching the forward troops chaos would quickly rear its repulsive head. Luckily, and due to a scheme put in hand during the winter of 1917/18, a stock of MT had been collected by GHQ in order to provide a strategic reserve to be deployed in an emergency. This was not a 'mothballing' exercise, all of the vehicles that were to form the reserve underwent a comprehensive overhaul to restore them to full operational order. At the same time, the practice of using MT in specific roles was abandoned in favour of a 'general usage' policy which greatly increased the operational utility of the available vehicles. In order to save the roads for use in a future campaign, the light railways were operated to the fullest extent possible and standard gauge lines were extended to the point where HT could collect supplies directly from the trains. But as the Fates were to decree, both light and standard gauge railheads were lost in large numbers during the ferocious onslaughts of the enemy. As the last fully functioning assets, for a time, virtually the whole of the BEF's supply services were thrust upon the shoulders of MT.

The French as well as the BEF had become adept in the use of MT, experience gained at Verdun in 1916 when lorries had saved the day, was put to good use in the spring of 1918. At one hour's notice, 100,000 men, plus artillery pieces for three divisions and their horses were moved 190 miles.

The workings of bus companies had also received attention. Auxiliary Omnibus Companies had been formed by GHQ for the same strategic reasons that applied to the lorries. A high proportion of the buses were discovered to be in a parlous state of disrepair and required a great deal of skilled work to make them fit to render reliable service. Many exercises to practise swift boarding by large bodies of troops had taken place. Bus stops were erected and allotted to twenty-five men. A brigade of 3,500 men could be lifted in as little as six minutes, the equivalent today of fifty double deck buses. As to loading them all in six minutes...?

With Fifth Army staggering under the enemy assault, a critical gap began to open with their neighbours, the French Sixth Army. If the gap had been allowed to develop the enemy would have very soon driven a wedge between the Allies, command and control would have collapsed (as it did twenty-two years later), the Germans would have raced for the French coast cutting north-south communications as they advanced. Fortunately for the Allies, at the critical moment, the humble motor bus was to hand. Whole divisions or parts of, were rushed at short notice to reinforce the line and stem the enemy who were pouring through the gap like a spring tide.

As an example of the speed and efficiency of the bus companies, on the night of 23/24 March, 12th Division was moved from Busnes to the town of Albert on the Somme to plug a gap in the line where a strong enemy attack was developing. The distance travelled as the crow flies was 48 miles (77 kilometres); the actual mileage was probably greater as the column would have travelled via the correct road circuits. The division went on to stall the German attack just west of Albert. The ASC bus drivers performed a magnificent service at a time of great danger, conveying 211,213 troops and often going without sleep for two-and-a-half days.

Lorries were in great demand, so much so that they were sent back against the flow of retreating men in order to salvage ammunition that had been abandoned. By so doing large amounts of ammunition was

More scrap vehicles 1918 – every re-usable part was removed. (Courtesy of R. Pullen)

denied to the enemy that could have been used with captured guns. To drive a soft-skinned vehicle towards an advancing enemy and within the range of his artillery, must have taken consummate nerve.

The 18th (Eastern) Division had a reputation as one of the finest in the BEF, renowned for its fighting spirit and good organisation. The division was in action for the greater part of the final eight months of the war with logistics supplied by 18th Divisional MT Company. The following is an extract from the company's war diary which can be found in full at the National Archives. It conveys in somewhat terse prose, the daily life of the company in those dark days:

1 March 1918, Railhead at Appilly – Divisional strength, 11,486 & 2715 horses – 21 lorries in use plus 2 on postal service, 4 to GHQ Agricultural Company & 1 to Noyon for sundries.

18th Division; hard fighting from 21-26th March finally retreating to the West of the Crozat canal.

26th March. Railhead at Estrees-St.-Dennis, Column on the move – leave Ribecourt for Jonquieres for overnight stop. Divisional strength 14,152 & 5645 horses – one Triumph motor cycle No.277360 captured by the enemy.

NO motor cycle has performed better service at the front ; ask the despatch rider

Every TRIUMPH produced during the past four years has gone to the battle areas. The test of war has confirmed its Speed & Strength ; its Reliability

For the days of peace there will be no motor cycle superior to the TRIUMPH

**Triumph Cycle Co. Ltd
Coventry**

Advertisement for 'Triumph' motor cycle.

2nd April, Railhead at Amiens, leave Hebecourt for position on Amiens to Poix road just outside Saleuel. 21 lorries on ammunition – 15 lorries on supplies – 2 lorries on post – 18 lorries on ammunition detachment to Amiens –15 of 3-ton lorries arrive from A.B.H.A.P.S.

18th Division; counter attack by the division on ridge North of Aubercourt repulsed with heavy loss – hard fighting during the whole of April.

5th May, Railhead at Poulainville, Divisional strength 17,826 & 4145 horses – 8 lorries on ammunition – 33 lorries on supplies – 2 on post – 10 on road stone –2 on coal.

The diary reveals that the strength of 18th Division actually increased by 6,340 men between 1 March and 5 May. Over the same period, the number of horses also increased by 1,430. Also, of important note was the multi-role utilisation of the lorries – anything, anywhere, anytime now being the rule instead of the exception.

Division holding the line opposite Albert.

18th May, railhead at Poulainville, Divisional Strength, 15,628 & 3913 horses, 21 lorries on ammunition – 33 lorries on supplies – 2 lorries on post – remained here till mid-July on routine supply operations. Pte. Cox transferred to K.S.L.I. [King's Shropshire Light Infantry] *reason, misconduct.*

In appreciation of the efforts of bus companies in those dangerous days, Sir Douglas Haig wrote:

Please convey to all ranks of the Auxiliary Omnibus Park my great appreciation of the services rendered by them since 21 March. The details of the work they have accomplished, in circumstances of peculiar hardship and difficulty, have been brought to my notice and constitute a record of which every officer and man may well be proud. They may rest assured that in meeting the heavy demands recently made upon them, through long hours of continual duty both on the road and in the workshops, they have greatly assisted the operations of our troops and have contributed in no small way to the frustration of the enemy's plans. I thank them for the work they have done, and count with confidence upon the same loyal service and devotion in the future.

A Radical Development in MT?

All flesh and blood creatures are susceptible to death and injury from flying splinters of hot metals. Add shrapnel bullets to the lethal mix and a very dangerous environment quickly emerges. A war of movement began to develop on the Western Front in the spring of 1918. To maintain momentum in any forward movement the troops needed far more in the way of supplies than they could possibly carry and at the same time remain effective. Another perennial problem was that of incoming hostile fire from the attacker's flanks, known as enfilade fire. The narrower the front, the greater was the danger of being caught in enfilade. The large numbers of horses and lorries that would be needed to re-supply the troops and keep up the tempo of the battle, would be targets of choice for the enemy. The standard alternative was to employ large numbers of men to carry water and ammunition, itself a task dangerous to the point of being almost beyond description. The solution lay in a self-powered vehicle, preferably running on tracks instead of wheels, and able to absorb at least some of the hurricane of metals hurled against it.

No such purpose-built tracked load carrier was available (there still isn't) but, a suggestion was put forward – why not use 'old' tanks? At the time, July 1918, no British heavy tank was more than twenty-two months old when plans were being laid for the Battle of Hamel. The 'old' tanks were those of the Mk I, II, III and some of the Mk IV type. All were of the classic rhomboid shape, size and weight, as was the new Mk V which had the distinct advantage of being fully driven by the driver, not as in the earlier models which required the efforts of four members of the crew to drive and manoeuvre it. Could the main battle tanks be spared for ASC work or was there a possible alternative?

Gun Carrier, converted for supply use.

Old tank converted for supply use (also towed sledges loaded with supplies.

But all was not lost; tracked 'Gun Carriers' which had been equipped with a field howitzer, became ready-made cross-country vehicles for the prompt delivery of food, water and ammunition to the Australian and American fighting troops at Le Hamel on 4 July 1918. Sledges were constructed to carry extra stores and be towed by the converted carriers. Each load weighing 12,500lbs, making a total of 50,000lbs, reached the forward troops within forty minutes of the capture of the enemy positions. Yet more water and ammunition was carried on the fighting tanks for the use of the infantry. Aircraft were also deployed in a novel role to parachute stores to the infantry.

Hamel was an 'all arms' battle and signified the beginning of the end of the war. The supply tanks replaced 1,200 men who would have had to struggle with heavy loads of approximately 41lbs each man, in the highly dangerous conditions of the battlefield. Had MT in the form of the carriers not been deployed, many of the human carriers would have become casualties and the forward troops would have quickly run out of supplies. Ninety minutes had been allotted for the entire operation; the troops and the fighting tanks arrived on the final objective in ninety-three minutes, a stunning achievement. The supply tank crews had yet another duty to perform, wounded soldiers were transported away from the battlefield on the carriers or the sledges. Not a comfortable or very quick ride at 4 mph at most, but at least they were travelling in the right direction towards help and relative safety. Returning fighting tanks also conveyed wounded in the spirit of 'good fellowship' as laid down in a tank training manual S.S. 204 of April 1918; Infantry and Tank co-operation and Training' which stressed the vital importance of infantry and tank co-operation.

Why include carrier tanks in the story of MT? The answer is a short one, most of the original tank drivers who deployed to France with the first machines used in September 1916, were ASC drivers and it is not unreasonable to assume that some of the original lads were still driving in 1918.

'Old' tanks were used as carriers in the battles of the Hundred Days from August to November 1918. Major W.L. Watson, an Oxford history graduate who served as a tank company commander, published a remarkable memoir of his experiences during those memorable times, *A Company of Tanks* vividly describes life in a tank carrier company. Although the tank men were members of the Tank Corps, they were fulfilling the role of the ASC. Under manned, everyone was expected to pitch in from the major to the cook. The old tanks were in a sorry state but by means of herculean efforts by all ranks, including the procurement and fitting of new engines, the 'old buses' were transformed from, 'breakdowns waiting to happen' to reliable supply carriers. Major Watson tells us that his crews took supplies of all kinds right up to the fighting infantry as the battles raged where wheeled transport of any kind could not reach. Tanks would swing round to present their sides, often in full view of the enemy, so acting as a shield for the unloaders. In so doing, crew members were killed, wounded and/or gassed, profoundly illustrating that the work of supply was no sinecure. In short, men, horses or lorries could not have faced those conditions and survived, as Major Watson related:

> *It became increasingly difficult for us to convince ourselves that we were not fighting troops. We had followed the infantry 'over the top'; we had dumped supplies in full view of the enemy; one of my tanks had received a direct hit, and had been set on fire; another tank had been abandoned practically in*

No-Mans-Land because every man in the crew had become a casualty; a third tank with a Highland Colonel on board, had started to mop up a machine-gun nest. We began to wonder whether, after all, we were a fit receptacle for 'crocks'. And we did not forget that Carrier Tanks were manned only by skeleton crews, and that in consequence, every member of the crew was driven to work day and night. An Australian General recommended one of my section commanders for a decoration, and at the first opportunity sent by his car a present to the section of two jars of rum and a few cases of chocolate.

Note: Carrier tanks were armed with one forward firing machine gun by utilising the forward gun mount from the tank's fighting days.

On the previously mentioned subject of whisky Watson recalled:

Mac, of all reconnaissance officers the most conscientious, had spent a whole night accompanied by his orderly in finding a route through difficult country to Bonnay. In the course of their nocturnal wanderings they came upon a mysterious camp, deserted yet full of stores. Amongst which were several cases of whiskey. I can think of no greater tribute to the discipline of the Tank Corps than the fact that Mac, after making a note of this important discovery, did not linger in the tent for even a moment, but went out into the night.

Note: Where at all possible, tank approach routes were planned with meticulous precision. When all the observation flaps were closed, vision from heavy tanks was severely restricted. White tapes laid on the ground could be used but often got chewed up by the first tank to pass over them. Often, the bravest of the brave, a section officer, would stand out in the open and point to the tank's objective.... many were killed.

A tracked supply vehicle capable of carrying a 3-ton load was designed by a Colonel Newton. Contracts were signed for 22,000 of these machines but none came into service before the end of the war. Also, of note was the development of the Mk IX supply tank, capable of carrying 10 tons of stores or thirty men, plus, the machine could tow three sledges. Unfortunately, although this tank showed great promise,

Mk IX Personnel and supply carrier tank – too late to see service.

only one was ever delivered to the front-line supply units. The Mk V Star, a longer version of the standard British heavy tank was designed as a fighting tank that could also transport twenty-five infantrymen. Unfortunately, due to extreme motion sickness and the effects of fumes, when the infantrymen regained fresh air, they were most often rendered incapable of any action, offensive or defensive. There is a case on record in which a group of infantrymen who upon disembarking from a tank declared: *'Never again, from now on we stay outside and die like gentlemen.'*

The Battle of Amiens, The Black Day of the German Army

'The invader has recoiled. His effectives are falling, his morale is weakening, whilst on our side our American comrades have already made our disconcerted enemy feel the vigour of their blows. Today I say to you, with tenacity, boldness and vigour, victory must be yours.'

These are the resounding words of Field Marshal Ferdinand Foch (1851-1929) spoken on 7 August 1918, the eve of the Battle of Amiens. At the instigation of Field Marshal Sir Douglas Haig, Foch had been appointed Supreme Commander of all Allied forces on the Western Front on Tuesday, 26 March 1918. Haig did not trust Marshal Pétain to be in overall command '*as he (Petain) had a terrible look, he had the appearance of a Commander who was in a funk and had lost his nerve.*' Twenty-two years later, Pétain as head of a provisional government, surrendered to the invading Germans. Foch had begun his military career at the age of 19 at the time of the Franco-Prussian War although he did not take an active part in the fighting. At war's end in 1871 Foch returned to his native city of Metz in the area of Alsace which was occupied by German soldiers, as the terms of the peace treaty ceded the whole territory of Alsace-Lorraine to Germany. Foch made a vow to himself that one day the lost territories would be restored to France. At the time of his appointment to Supreme Commander, Foch was 67 years old, Haig was ten years younger at 57.

Thursday, 8 August 1918, a day without the least importance to most people today, but this was the day that irrevocably sealed the fate of Germany. Known to history as the Battle of Amiens, this was to be a repeat of the 'all arms' assault of Le Hamel on a much larger scale. The battle was mainly fought by Fourth Army commanded by General Sir Henry Rawlinson (Rawly, the Fox) who had long held to his belief that although troops on the Western Front could 'break in', 'breakthrough' was not possible. The Fox was a proponent of the doctrine of 'bite and hold', that is attack the enemy in overwhelming strength then, when resistance begins to harden, as it did so two days later, to close down the battle and deliver another smashing blow elsewhere and repeat. In effect this is exactly the tactic used by the Allies. In trying to defend against the blows, the Germans were forced to rely upon their already crumbling transport and supply system, a situation that only worsened as each day passed up to the Armistice. For the BEF, with its highly developed logistical arm, such changes to the point of attack could be carried out with relative ease.

General Ludendorff, the de-facto head of the German Army, suffered a heart attack on 8 August and referred to that date as the '*Black Day of the German Army*'.

As in every detail of the First World War, there are no absolutes. In the autumn of 1918, tanks were operating in devasted country where MT could not reach. Ironically, HT came to the rescue, delivering all the needs of the tanks and their crews, including petrol. As an example, the Mk V tank was supposed to have a petrol consumption of 2 gallons per mile, in reality, in the devastated areas petrol was 'guzzled' at the rate of 12 gallons per mile. MT brought the petrol forward from the nearest working Head of Steel to the ends of usable roads, whereupon HT worked the dangerous liquid forward. For the ASC the work load became even greater. The reader will note the war diaries often quote the numbers of men and horses serving in divisions; these figures represented the rations to be drawn from the railheads, no more and no less, the control of waste was paramount.

> *2nd August, Railhead at Poulainville, Divisional Strength, 19,376 & 4921 horses, 44 lorries on ammunition – 4 on supplies – 2 lorries on post – 1 lorry to driving school. 18th Division plans for 8 August attack revealed to battalion commanders.*
>
> *30th August, Railhead at Edge Hill (Rancourt) 48 lorries on ammunition – 4 lorries on supplies –2 lorries on post – 1 lorry to Y.M.C.A. Amiens – 2 lorries on 3rd Corps Water Column. 18th Division; the division re-captured Trones Wood on the Somme repeating their success of 1916 in the same location.*

Also, once again in action 256 Coy. *When BEF advanced beyond Arras, lorries engaged for several days conveying heavy bridge building material, often under heavy shell fire, forward to Monchy le Preux & Tilloy.*

The importance of salvage at all times – in his final despatch of March 1919:

> *Sir Douglas Haig recorded that in August 1918, the BEF recovered 860,000lbs of dripping which was sent back to the UK. While the cash value of the by-products disposed of from all sources has exceeded £60,000 (£3,539,532) in a single month. Provision was made for baths and a new Inspectorate supervised the running of Army laundries on up-to-date lines.'*
>
> *1st September, the 18th Division has captured Combles.*
>
> *8th September, Railhead at Trones Wood, 45 lorries on ammunition.*
>
> *11th September, Railhead at Trones Wood, Divisional strength, 14049 & 3731 horses, 35 lorries on ammunition – 11 lorries on supplies – 1 lorry on salvage – 1 lorry to Y.M.C.A. Amiens – 1 lorry to Paris for pumping equipment.*

18th Division is out of the line for rest and training. (Author's note – date not shown, division was only out of the line for four days.)

18th September, Division in hard fighting for the Hindenburg outpost lines.

19th September, Railhead at Quincunxes (sic) 21 lorries on salvage collected from divisional area.

With some daring to dream that the end of the war might soon become a reality, the business of keeping the Army moving had to go on as the partially quoted letter of 19 September 1918, from Fourth Army HQ enquiring as to the parlous state of a unit's lorries demonstrates:

I am informed that 14th & 21st Brigades Royal Garrison Artillery had 33% of its lorries immobile....It is considered that this percentage of immobile lorries (if Correct) is abnormally high....Will you kindly obtain for me a report on this matter?

It has also been brought to my notice that 27.5% of the lorries of 5th, 14th, 23rd & 298th Royal Field Artillery or Royal Horse Artillery ammunition parks were immobile on transfer to 1X Corps.... Kindly report on this matter as well.

Signed E. Gillespie, B.G. (Brigadier General) D.D.S.& T. (Deputy Director Supplies & Transport) Fourth Army.

A communication of this nature would turn the recipient's veins to ice. This was a very serious matter, as all MT was urgently required, and excuses would not be accepted, in exceptional circumstances, 'a good reason' just might be. The lorries were needed urgently, 1,600 lorries had a carrying capacity equal to a double line of railway but only on regular journeys of 37-50 miles, on occasional journeys of 90-100 miles the lorry became less efficient and more so as greater distances were involved.

22nd September, 6 lorries carrying walking wounded.
23/24th September, Division still engaged in heavy fighting for the Hindenburg outposts.

(Author's note – on a line Épehy–Ronssoy–Templeux-le-Guérard, the contested posts themselves being known *as* Duncan, Doleful, Egg and

Tambois Farm, all circa 14 miles (22 kilometres) just south-west from Cambrai.)

27th September, Railhead at Plateau, 6 lorries carrying walking wounded.

28 September we again find 256 Coy. *'Lorries standing by with Pontoons for Bourlon Wood (near Cambrai) and delivered to Triangle Dump, Hedecourt* (sic). The pontoons were probably for use in crossing the nearby Canal du Nord.

Following the Battle of Amiens on 8 August, the Allies, at the behest of Marshal Foch, launched a series of crushing attacks upon the invader. These attacks have become known to history as the Battles of the Hundred Days in which, all of the industrial might of the Allies was now concentrated with the single objective of bringing about the total defeat of the enemy.

As the battle front moved eastwards, so the BEF's lines of communication became extended. Until the railway construction troops could repair the lines destroyed by the enemy – and in many cases push new lines forward which, to their eternal credit, they accomplished at breakneck speeds – MT could be found 'running the loops' from railheads 50 miles behind the front lines, requiring a round trip of 100 miles. Driver fatigue increased rapidly, as did the amount of petrol needed to sustain forward movement. The troops always and without fail had to be properly fed and supplied with small arms ammunition. The ever-hungry guns also clamoured for their far heavier, gas, smoke, shrapnel and high explosive shells. Artillery was now 'Queen of the Battlefield' and prime protector of the infantry and, as mentioned before in this work, the ASC had made it a point of honour not to let the lads down under any circumstances.

On 29 September, General Sir Henry Rawlinson launched five army corps against the enemy's Hindenburg Line, between St Quentin and Cambrai in company with 175 tanks. By the end of the first day the first and second lines of the Hindenburg Line had fallen on a front of 5 miles; on the fifth day, the enemy's third line fell leading Rawlinson to note in his diary: *'The 2nd Australian and British 25th Division broke through the Hindenburg Line and my leading troops are out in the open, so my victory is won.'*

In order to achieve that which the Tank Corps quantified as *'From mud through blood to the green fields beyond'*, the Royal Artillery consumed in the 24 hours, noon on 28 September to noon on 29 September, 943,847 rounds. Earlier we mentioned 'break in' was all that was possible, now with the advent of the all arms battle, 'breakthrough' was being achieved. The 29 September attack is now largely forgotten by mainstream history, and with it, the major role in the stunning success played by the ASC. Major M. de B. Scott, of the ASC wrote of the dilemma facing the BEF and in particular the ASC and its fleet of motor lorries.

By 1 October, the BEF entered a district from which the Germans had forcibly removed all men of military age or, those who could be used in manufacturing industry. In the zone of France near the border with Belgium the British discovered 790,000 people in desperate need of food and medical supplies of whom, in the district of Lille, Roubaix and Tourcoing, were 450,000 people without food. Throughout the BEF area of operations (the war was still being bitterly fought) the civilian population was fed as agreed with the French Government, for a period of four days. Supplies of meat and flour arrived for Lille and were safely delivered by the ASC. The lorries operated by the ASC were a source of deliverance to the abandoned civil population; 5,084,000 rations were distributed at a time when MT was hugely committed to supplying the fighting fronts. The BEF through its ASC and MT assets was instrumental in saving from starvation at least 400,000 French people whom the Germans had systematically deprived of all means of subsistence. On 13 October, the BEF's 66th Division, facing the town of Le Cateau, became aware that the citizens of the town were near starvation and still in the grip of the invader. In an effort to succour the people of Le Cateau, the division arranged an 'air drop' of rations marked *'Habitants du Cateau, Envoi de la Armies Britannique'* demonstrating yet again the largely forgotten ingenuity of the BEF and the commitment of the ASC.

6th October, 256 Coy recorded: 'Pontoons delivered to various bridgeheads on the Canal d' Escaut. Several times the lorries advanced with the infantry & delivered pontoons while under machine gun fire and the conduct of all concerned was commended by the Chief Royal Engineers, Canadian Corps.'

> *15th October, Railhead at Epehy, 10 lorries on baggage –*
> *unknown number shown on ammunition build up. Column*
> *moves to Le Catelet (12½ miles 20 kilometres south of*
> *Cambrai.)*
>
> *18th October, 18th Division final advance commences from*
> *Le Cateau in a North easterly direction.*
>
> *20th October, railhead at Bohain, 66th Division relieved the*
> *18th concentrate at Le Cateau.*
>
> *22nd October, Railhead at Bellicourt.*
>
> *29th October, Railhead at Bellicourt, Divisional strength,*
> *12270 & 3964 horses, 19 lorries on ammunition – 30 lorries*
> *on supplies – 7 lorries on Royal Engineers detachment – 8*
> *lorries on stores – 2 lorries on post – 1 lorry on laundry.*
>
> *31st October, Railhead at Basigny, 48 lorries on ammunition.*

In mid-October, a short article appeared in the British press to the effect that there were those in Germany who had come to realise that the war was lost. An article published in a Strasburg newspaper announced the:

> *Formation of a German company to organise tours in the*
> *Vosges region after the war. It was claimed that the company*
> *had the backing of a large banking house. The hotel industry*
> *was to be reorganised and a system of integrated motor*
> *services (MT) would take visitors to the battlefields.*

The British article voiced serious reservations about the scheme; the recently fought over area was 'hallowed ground', at the same time it was realised that many families would, if it were possible, visit the graves or the last known place where their loved ones had fought. Seeing the need for guide books to the devastated areas, the Michelin Company was soon producing excellent guides to the battlefields for those who could afford to travel by car. Responding to the call for the less monied to visit the battlefields, in 1928 the British Legion (then without the prefix Royal) organised a mass tour at a price that many more could afford. The main means of conveyance for the thousands who joined the 'pilgrimage' was the railway but, not to be left out MT in the form of private cars and taxis were mobilised to take those whose relatives had been lost beyond walking distance from the disembarkation point of the railway, to visit sites especially important and sacred to them. It may also be of interest for readers to know that British publications anticipated battlefield visits and restoration of the devasted areas as early as the autumn of 1915. Lorries were to be utilised in the restoration of farms, villages and towns. Char-a-bancs would provide for the needs of the high numbers of sightseers as well as those who would come to mourn their lost loved ones.

As the battle moved eastwards the country was laid waste by the retreating enemy. Crossroads were mined by delayed-action devices requiring members of the Royal Engineers to locate and render them harmless. Bridges were destroyed, trees felled to block roads, private houses wrecked and their contents stolen or burnt, orchards destroyed, wells poisoned, livestock driven away and foodstuffs stolen in an orgy of theft and destruction. MT was forced to find long detours on unfamiliar roads and lanes in the hope of avoiding land mines. In many cases, a day's run extended to three days, leading to the slowing of the Army's advance. Hence the diary entry below.

1ˢᵗ November, as above, 51 lorries on ammunition – 2 lorries on pack saddles [to enable HT to replenish supplies in the devastated areas where 'wheels' could not reach]

2ⁿᵈ November, 20 lorries on bridging materials.

3ʳᵈ November, Railhead at Bohain.

4ᵗʰ November, Railhead at Montbrehain, 32 lorries on supplies – 13 on ammunition.

7ᵗʰ November, Railhead at Bellicourt, 64 lorries on supplies – 5 lorries on baggage – 3 lorries on trench mortar stores.

11ᵗʰ November 1918, Railhead at Bellicourt, Divisional strength, 12376 & 2638 horses, no lorries on ammunition – 24 lorries on supplies – 2 lorries on post – 2 lorries on laundry – 2 lorries on coal – 5 lorries on various duties. Hostilities will cease at eleven o' clock – the Company moved from Moret to Le Cateau, parking up in the Boulevard Paturle.

So, with only a terse comment, the ASC's active part in the Great War came to an end.

Town square, Lille, 1918.

Chapter 11

A Brave New World?

The war was over, or was it? An armistice is a temporary cessation of hostilities; the war itself did not officially end until 28 June 1919 with the signing of the Treaty of Versailles. Millions of civilians who were attired in soldiers' uniforms were clamouring for release in order to take up their family life and employment. Unfortunately, the world of 1914 had largely disappeared; the large estates which had been the source of much employment in rural areas had lost many of the heirs to the land. Most of the manufacturing capacity of the UK had been given over to war work and would take a long time to revert to peacetime operations. Overseas markets for manufactured goods had been disrupted leading customers to seek their needs elsewhere. Even 'King Coal' was in difficulties which a few years later resulted in mass unemployment in Britain's coalfields.

ASC lorries at Cambrai railway station, 1918.

'Dunlop Rubber Co.' end of war advertisement.

For the ASC, on 12 November 1918 the work of supply and salvage went on without a pause. The front lines had to be maintained and at the same time, a new service came into being – the rescue of destitute civilians from the country occupied by the invader. In many cases, these poor souls had had everything they owned looted; some were discovered without as much as a single blanket or a crust of bread; men, women, young and old, none had been spared.

On 27 November a Royal Warrant, published in Army Orders, states that the King, *'having noted with great satisfaction the splendid work which has been performed by our Army Service Corps and our Army Veterinary Corps during the present war, has ordained that in future they shall enjoy the distinction of "Royal."'* A similar honour was conferred upon the Army Ordnance Corps for the same reason.

An anonymous war diary recorded:

Over a 4-day period 5 lorries each day conveying civilians.
25th November, 2 lorries loaded with blankets
2nd December, 35 lorries on supplies and 1 to Church Army
25th December, 15 lorries on supplies, 3 on coal, 15 on other duties
1st January 1919, 42 lorries on the road
30th April 1919, 31 lorries on the road plus 4 on salvage, 2 on supplies

Each day throughout this period two lorries were always allotted to the Army Postal Service.

To set matters in context, the ASC had 2,700,000 soldiers to feed. As Sir Douglas Haig remarked in his final despatch of 1919, *'an increase of one ounce in the overall soldier's ration was equal to 75 extra tons'* which in turn would require twenty 3-ton lorries to deliver that extra ounce. On supply, Sir Douglas commented:

> *It is hardly too much to assert that, however seemingly extravagant in men and money, no system of supply, except the most perfect should ever be contemplated. To give an example, unless our supply services had been fully efficient the great advance carried out by our Armies during the autumn of last year could not have been carried out. Wars may be won or lost by the standard of health and morale of the opposing force. Morale depends to a very large extent upon the feeding and general wellbeing of the troops.*

T.E. Lawrence (Lawrence of Arabia) remarked: '*The invention of bully-beef has modified land warfare more profoundly than the invention of*

ASC convoy, unknown location, 1918.

gunpowder.' 'Bully' was carried forward in enormous quantities by the ASC; good staple food that was not liable to damage by water and from which Tommy learned to produce a variety of different dishes, both in and out of the line.

Coming Home as seen by ASC cartoonist.

Due to the imminent demobilization of hundreds of thousands of troops, the all-important work of salvage was carried on at an accelerated pace. Unexploded shells were a particular menace but all the same, had to be dealt with. The *Lingo of No Man's Land* describes duds as follows:

> *Dud Shell: A dud shell is a dead one; that is, one which does not explode on being fired. Removing these unexploded shells is one of the dangers of reclaiming waste land over which the armies have been fighting, as they sometimes explode unexpectedly when struck by a rifle.*

Visitors to the Western Front will come across unexploded ammunition. Unexploded does not mean that the **shell will not explode**; do not, under any circumstances touch or handle these shells, they look rusty but inside they are as good as new and only waiting for the command signal to do that for which they were manufactured – to explode with devastating results.

A sad duty undertaken by MT was the transport of dead soldiers' effects. The press baron, Lord Northcliffe had noted as early as 1916 that the work went on throughout the war and for some time thereafter. Even today, if effects are found with the remains of a British soldier, they are, when possible, returned to his nearest living relative. The earliest search for effects were carried out on the battlefield where they were listed then sent back to one of the large rear bases; here they would be checked again before being placed in a bag for transport to the next of kin.

Next of kin obviously treasured these items but some became indignant when an item sent to their relative was not among the effects received and who in their towering grief, lashed out at the army department in France that had despatched the items. One such letter was quoted by Northcliffe: *'I gave my son to the war, you have had him, you might at least return all his property intact. Where are the pair of gloves and zinc ointment, he had with him?'*

To the end of its time in France and Flanders, the ASC would have been responsible for at least a part of the carriage of these very sad consignments destined for those who would have to shoulder the intolerable burden of grief for the remainder of their days. How then was it for those who would never knew the whereabouts of their loved one? For them there would only be the small consolation of the numerous memorials to the missing that stretch in a long line through Belgium and France. It may be of interest to readers that Lord Northcliffe mentions 'Watchers':

> *It was an obvious step to install Watchers in all hospitals. These watchers were given lists of names of missing men, and it was their duty to ask new patients if they knew anything of these men, to note down their answers in the smallest detail and to forward them to headquarters.*

Northcliffe went on to relate the story of a 'missing' soldier who turned up some time later, working as an army cook, a duty that he had been legally posted to. The 'system' itself had lost this soldier, but the joy of his family would have been boundless. The author recalls a case from Knowle in Warwickshire in which a local land agent received a tap on the shoulder, to be informed that he had been buried at Gallipoli. 'I picked some wild flowers and placed them on your grave', said his informant. Who the occupant of the grave could be, no one will ever know.

'Associated Equipment Company' [AEC] lorries for disposal, 1919.

The Nail Collector

The final year of the war witnessed the introduction of a 'Nail Collector' into the vast array of equipment used by the BEF. The signed blue-print shown here reveals the BEF's answer to the horseshoe nail problem; the collector was made in-house from parts acquired or manufactured locally. Rechargeable batteries powered electro-magnets which attracted any ferrous metal on or near the road surface. An iron scoop would be placed under the machine and the current to the magnets switched off causing the ferrous debris to fall onto the scoop from whence all the recovered material was sent to salvage. Probably without knowing the reason why, many a driver was spared the labour and frustrating delays caused by punctures. The ears of other road users would have also been spared the streams of invective hurled by the drivers against tyres and the world in general as, in order to repair the damage, they wrestled with freezing hands, often in sticky mud and puddles of water and, in rain propelled by the ever-searching wind.

This rather strange looking machine came about due to the increased use of pneumatic tyres, in particular for cars and motor cycles. Due to the presence of millions of horseshoe nails on the roads, multiple punctures were a fact of life and had been so prior to the war. Owners

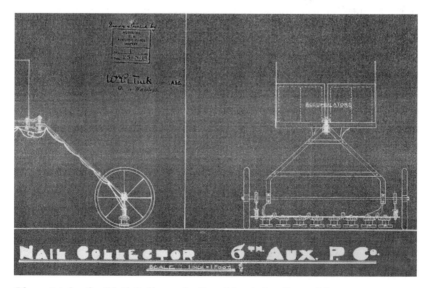

Blueprint for the 'Nail Collector' – Royal Logistics Corps Museum.

had been offered numerous 'cures' for the incessant, time and money consuming punctures including, filling the tyre with foam, fitting a 'multi' inner tube which was supposed to work on the principle that all of the tubes would not fall victim to the nails. The foam filling would heat up as the vehicle was driven then, when the vehicle was parked, the weight pressed down on the tyre causing the warm foam to produce a flat shape at the bottom of the wheel thereby rendering the whole wheel and tyre assembly useless. As for the multi-tube, yes all of the tubes could be punctured in short order. The price of a replacement for a standard inner tube to the BEF was 10s (£29.50) plus the valuable shipping space required to carry the rubber from the Far East in the face of the depredations of enemy submarines.

But MT was not alone from suffering mishaps due to horseshoe nails as a notice proclaimed: **'Pick Up A Nail and Save A Horse'.** These notices were accompanied by biscuit tins into which passer-by would deposit any nails found, these nails were sent for salvage, either for re-use or scrap metal. A horse made lame by treading on a nail had to be taken off the road immediately, prolonged veterinary care could be involved while the unfortunate horse still had to have his rations.

Aftermath

Following the official end of the war in 1919, the UK Government found itself in possession of thousands of surplus vehicles of all types. The only reasonable course of action to take instead of cutting the vehicles up for scrap was to sell them as going concerns. A great many men and women had acquired driving skills across a wide range of MT. Plus, there existed a large body of newly unemployed fitters and mechanics. Discharged soldiers purchased ex-government lorries in order to try their luck, often converting the lorry to a charabanc at weekends to obtain maximum revenue from their investment. So was born out of the fires of war, the seemingly unstoppable rise of MT.

On 14 February 1920, King George V, for the very first time, set foot upon an omnibus, the bus in question being B43 or 'Old Bill' of the Menin Road. Old Bill had been invited to Buckingham Palace together with forty employees of the London General Omnibus Company who all wore their medal ribbons on their dark blue company uniforms. Old Bill had served faithfully in France and Flanders and was selected as part of a batch of 150 omnibuses for return to the UK for complete refurbishment and return to revenue-earning service on the streets of London. Gone was the grey paintwork and boarded up windows of the battle area, Old Bill was once more resplendent in bright red paintwork. Not a speck of dust was to be seen, the only visible sign that the bus had seen long and active service was a brass plaque detailing its battle honours, Antwerp–Ancre–Somme–Amiens–Home. His Majesty shook hands with all the employees and took a keen interest in the bus itself.

Right*: Daimler Company souvenir awarded post war.* (Courtesy of R. Pullen)

Below*: Ex War Department lorry begins a new life in 1920.* (Courtesy of R. Pullen)

Of the Battle of Antwerp in 1914, the London General Omnibus Company house magazine published the following brief account of the part played by their employees and buses:

The Motor bus in Antwerp did a great work and all credit is due. The drivers absolutely kept the pot boiling the whole time by their incessant labour in feeding the trenches with ammunition and food, not to say the handling of the wounded. The coolness of the drivers under a veritable hail of shell and shrapnel fire was an outstanding feature of the fellows who had the good fortune to get through will have cause to be ever grateful for the manner in which our wonderful fleet assisted them. It was a sad sight to see the dear old buses battered about by the roadside as we left them in our retirement.

B43 Old Bill was donated to the Imperial War Museum in 1970. He was driven there, fittingly, by 80-year-old former driver George Gwynn, a veteran of bus driving on the Western Front. Driver Alfred Cummins was believed to be the last man alive to have driven a bus on the Western Front. He ended his days living comfortably in a London Transport Residential Home – 'once a busman always a busman'.

Thornycroft lorry converted to a bus finds itself working post war in Southampton.

Where to find a memorial to the ASC on the Western Front; this writer has never been able to discover a permanent memorial. Should a reader pay a visit to the Somme, they could drive the lorry routes shown on the Road Circuit Map, living memorials to those tumultuous days of long ago. Park up safely off road and pause to listen, you may just hear carried on the wind, the sound of a Thornycroft or a Daimler running one last loop up the line. Wish them well.

Richard Pullen intends to build a Thornycroft, so far, he has two hub caps...

Appendix 1

Technical details of the Nail Collector probably completed May 1918

DETAILS OF THE NAIL COLLECTOR.

Two pneumatic tyred cycle wheels, mounted on a light steel axle, carry the collecting part of the apparatus. Adjustably suspended from this axle is a steel bar on which the electro-magnets are mounted. The supports of this bar are free to swing on the axle, so that on the magnets hitting an obstacle, the whole bar swings backwards and upwards to clear the obstacle. The suspension of the magnet carrying bar is cushioned by short spiral springs. Each electro-magnet - of which there are eight - consists of a coil of insulated wire round a steel core. At the lower end of each steel core is a short cross-piece. It is to this cross-piece that the nails picked up adhere.

The suspension of the magnets is so arranged as to give an air space of 1" to 1¼" between the bottom of the cross pieces and the surface of the road.

The coils used in the apparatus made at Boulogne were old field windings from a C.A.V. lighting dynamo. Each of the coils is composed of about 180 yards of 21 S.W.G. copper insulated wire, giving about 600 turns in the coil.

Each coil is connected in series with another, each pair of serially-connected coils in parallel with the other pairs.

This apparatus is attached centrally to the back of a horse drawn wagon by a triangular frame of light steel bars. At Boulogne, a Wagon, light spring, has been found very suitable.

The power required to energize the electro-magnets is obtained from two sets of 12 bolt.car lighting accumulators (120 ampere-hours) which are carried in the wagon. The cells are connected in series.

There is a small switchboard on the side of the wagon, which distributes the current to each pair of magnets through tumbler switches.

The method of use is to draw the apparatus along the road, with an attendant walking behind. About every 50 or 60 yards, the wagon is stopped, and the attendant places a light iron scoop underneath each pair of magnets in turn, switches off the current, whereupon the nails, or any other iron collected, drop off into the scoop. The scoop is then emptied into a receptacle on the wagon, the current is switched on again, and the wagon proceeds.

No nails or small pieces of iron or steel are everypassed over without being picked up, nor can they be shaken off until the current is interrupted.

It is found that satisfactory results are obtained with the following hours of working and charging :-

Hours of work.	7.45 a.m. to 11.45 a.m.	4
	2.30 p.m. to 4.30 p.m.	2
Charge from	11.45 a.m. to 2.30 p.m. at 7 amperes	2¾
	4.30 p.m. to 7.45 a.m. at 5 amperes.	15¼
	Total charging hours..........	18

The working hours could be lengthened by using accumulators of bigger capacity and which would also stand a higher charging rates

Appendix 2

ASC examples of order sheets

Appendix 3

Illustrating the Power of Industry

During active operations, ammunition consumption was colossal, the production figures for the Kynoch works in Birmingham during March 1918 quoted here, convey a picture of the national effort being made by Great Britain to sustain her forces in the field. Kynochs were contracted to supply each week: 25,000,000 rifle cartridges, 300,000 revolver cartridges, 500,000 cartridge clips, 110,000 18-pounder brass cartridge cases and 300 tons of the explosive 'cordite'.

Yet more output was called for in order for the BEF to deal with the enemy offensive beginning March 1918. Responding to the emergency, in one week, Kynochs produced 29,750,000 rifle cartridges, all of which were manufactured to tolerances of +/-0.001 inches. The true picture emerges when the 102 individual operations required to form each of the above cartridges is considered: the total of operations reached 3,034,500,000, a truly staggering figure.

From a pre-war production figure of 135 Lee Enfield rifles per week, the Birmingham Small Arms Company (BSA) in less than two years were producing 10,000 Lee Enfields and, 2,000 Lewis Guns per week, plus many other war items in their hundreds of thousands each week.

The vast majority of this productive effort would pass through the hands of the ASC and be carried on the roads of France and Belgium. We must remind ourselves that the figures quoted above are only that of two factories. Great Britain contained thousands of similar enterprises great and small. Without his arms, the soldier becomes a liability but still needs food at 3,500 calories per day; not forgetting the horses, without fodder they quickly lose the ability to work and rapidly waste away. The enormous efforts of the home population and the ASC saw to it that our armies were kept fully equipped and well fed.

The military historian, Major General, J.F.C. Fuller, quantified the whole war as '*the battle between the German Ruhr valley and the British West Midlands, the latter won*'.

Appendix 4

The Army Service Corps
The resting places of those who lost their lives circle the globe

The total number of ASC deaths in service during the Great War recorded by the Commonwealth War Graves Commission (CWGC) is 9,460 commemorated across twenty-five countries.

As in all branches of the military in the years 1914-19 death came in many forms. Those who served the Corps did not share the constant danger of their infantry comrades, but they were certainly exposed to the reality of wounds or violent death in the course of their duties.

The number of those who died while serving in France and Flanders, the term used by the (CWGC) to record burials or commemoration in France and Belgium and the area covered by this work, is 3,878. Those who died in Germany total 13 possibly as prisoners of war or in the Army of Occupation. Deaths in the United Kingdom came to 2,913.

Many of the soldiers who served in the ASC were not fully fighting fit, but either recovering from wounds or classed as fit to serve but not in the main combatant arms. Unfortunately, the less a soldier's level of fitness, the higher were the chances of death if stricken by disease. The British Expeditionary Force insisted on very high standards of hygiene at all times, whether in or out of the front lines, but disease knew no frontiers and was waiting to strike in all its spiteful forms.

Death could strike through pneumonia, tuberculosis, heart disease and malignant growths, to name but a few of his numerous guises. The year 1918 was to witness Death unleash his greatest ever assault on humanity in the form of a virulent strain of influenza that became known as 'Spanish Flu'. Estimates of death from the 'flu vary wildly from 40,000,000 to 100,000,000. Troops who by necessity lived cheek by jowl were very susceptible to the disease; in general, 10 to 20 per cent of those infected died. The author knew a former soldier who, following 'flu infection in 1918 was declared dead and about to be carried out for burial when, fortunately for him and to the great surprise of his bearers, he woke up! A strange side-effect of the 'flu was low educational attainment in areas that had seen widespread infection.

R.I.P.

Bibliography

Sun Tzu, The Art of War, first translated in the late eighteenth century.

The Royal Army Service Corps: A History of Transport and Supply in the British Army, Sir John Fortescue and Colonel R.H. Beadon, published by Cambridge University Press 1931

Memoirs of an Unconventional Soldier, Major-General J.F.C. Fuller, published by Ivor Nicholson & Watson 1936

The Old Contemptibles; Robin Neillands, published by John Murray 2004

Supplying War; Martin Van Creveld, first published by Cambridge University Press 1977

The Retreat from Mons, A. Corbett-Smith, Published by Cassell 1916

A History of the Army Ordnance Services, Major General A. Forbes, published by The Medici Society 1929

Lingo of No Man's Land, Lorenzo N. Smith, published by Jamieson 1918

Motors in a Nutshell, Captain S. Bramley-Moore MC, published by E & F. N. Spon 1919

The Training of Mechanical Transport Drivers During the Great War, Captain J.T. Reckitt, published by A.S.C., 1920

The Wipers Times, Captain F. Roberts, reprinted by Little Books Ltd, 2006

Into Battle, A Soldier's Diary of the Great War, John Glubb, published by Cassell 1978

Statistics of the Military Effort of the British Empire During the Great War, reprinted by Naval & Military Press 1999

The History of the Pneumatic Tyre, Eric Tomkins, published by Eastland Press 1981

The Business of War, I.F. Marcossan, originally published in 1918, reprinted by Forgotten Books 2012

Warfare and Armed Conflict, Michael Clodfelter, published by McFarland 2002

Supply in Modern War, Colonel D.C. Shaw, published by Faber & Faber 1938

Sir John French's Despatches, published by *The Graphic*, London 1914

The Great Munition Feat, George A.B. Dewar, published by Constable & Co. London 1921

Before Endeavours Fade, Rose E.B. Coombs MBE, first published 1976 by Battle of Britain Prints International

The Motor Bus in War, A. M. Beatson, first published 1918, reprint 2014 by Echo

Sir Eric Geddes: Business and Government in War and Peace, Keith Grieves, published by Manchester University Press, 1989

Elsie and Mairi Go to War, Diane Atkinson, published by Preface, 2009

Lady Under Fire on the Western Front, A. & H. Hollom, published by Pen & Sword, 2010

Sir Douglas Haig's Despatches, J.H. Boraston, first published by Dent & Sons, 1919

A Company of Tanks, Major W.L. Watson DCM DSO first published by William Blackwood & Sons, Edinburgh & London 1920

With Our Backs to the Wall, David Stevenson, first published by Allen Lane 2011

The Great War Generals on the Western Front, Robin Neillands, published by Robinson Publishing Ltd. 1999

The Private Papers of Douglas Haig 1914-1919, edited by Robert Blake, published by Eyre & Spottiswoode, London 1952

At the War, Lord Northcliffe, published by Hodder and Stoughton, London 1916

The Story of an Epic Pilgrimage, published by the British Legion 1928. Note, the appellation 'Royal' was granted in 1971.

Index